Becoming the
BRIDE
of Christ in the
LAST DAYS

Becoming the
BRIDE
of Christ in the
LAST DAYS

How Jesus Will Make the
Church Ready in the Endtimes

Haavard Sand

DESTINY IMAGE™ EUROPE srl
Via Maiella, 1
66020 San Giovanni Teatino (Ch) - Italy

"Changing the world, one book at a time!"

This book and all other Destiny Image™ Europe books are available at Christian bookstores and distributors worldwide.

To order products, or for any other correspondence:

DESTINY IMAGE™ EUROPE srl
Via Acquacorrente, 6
65123 - Pescara - Italy
Tel: +39 085 4716623 - Fax: +39 085 9431270
E-mail: info@eurodestinyimage.com

Or reach us on the Internet: **www.eurodestinyimage.com**

ISBN: 978-88-89127-70-4
For Worldwide Distribution, Printed in U.S.A.
1 2 3 4 5 6 7 8/13 12 11 10 09

ACKNOWLEDGMENTS

First of all I want to thank my wife, Karen. You are the bride God prepared for me and one who belongs to the bridal generation. It was the first edition of this book—which was published in the Philippines—that God sovereignly used to bring us closer together. This time we have edited again this book together (for the international edition) but now as husband and wife. You are an excellent editor, and this book would never have turned out so well without you. You are a great gift from God to me. Thank you for your love, intercession, encouragement, and support.

Sincere thanks to my family: my mom and dad, for believing in me and supporting me, even when I have chosen a different path in life in a country far away. To my brother Vebjorn, for generously supporting this book project financially. To Eimund, your encouragement for me to write this book was one of the important elements to get me started. Aune, for your continual love and care for David and me. To my sister Ane, I am proud to have you as a little sister who has grown up to be a beautiful and gifted woman. And to our son, David, for allowing me to spend so many hours away from you so I could work on the book. I love you, son.

Special thanks for all my friends who helped me with their input and comments: Ole Christian, Brian, James, and Aileen. Also my deep gratitude to all my friends and benefactors who prayed, encouraged, supported, and believed in the message God has given me in this book. I will be forever grateful to all of you. My deep appreciation to Dorte and Anton–for your continuous support and friendship, to Kjelli–for your special friendship and intercession, and to Moni–for your friendship to our family and your faithful support. And a special thanks to all who have contributed financially to the publishing of this international edition.

Thanks also to Frank Zakkariassen for his help. Lastly, I want to thank Mike Bickle for his God-given insights and revelations that have formed and influenced much of my thoughts and understanding of the Word.

Above all, thank You, Jesus. The One who is beauty and who made all things beautiful in His own time. Thank You, for Your wonderful love and care for me. Without You this book would never have been written. May Your beauty be displayed in all the earth. And let this simple attempt contribute to that. You deserve our highest praise and our utmost adoration.

ENDORSEMENTS

My recently published book, entitled *The World's Greatest Revivals,* concluded with the prophetic presumption that the essential rediscovered truth of the next major revival will be about the Bridegroom and the Bride, Jesus united with His Church in a loving, passionate relationship. Haavard Sand's book, *Becoming the Bride of Christ in the Last Days,* reflects that reality in a powerful way and thus will serve to pave the way in the Body of Christ for a growing bridal understanding of our relationship with Jesus, our Bridegroom.

Fred Wright
International Coordinator for Partners in Harvest

The Church is transforming into the Bride of Christ, ready to receive our Bridegroom Jesus and saying, with the Holy Spirit, "Come, Lord Jesus!" Haavard Sand persuasively argues that the transformation of the Church calls for restoring the first commandment and returning to a heavenly mindset. Night after night, my wife Doris and I have read this book together devotionally. We have been moved to embrace the passion awaiting the Bridegroom and to have the mind of Christ.

Luis Bush
International Facilitator, Transform World Connection

This very timely book, *Becoming the Bride of Christ in the Last Days*, by Haavard Sand is a powerful introduction to one of the most important end-time agendas: the preparation of the Church as the Bride of Christ. In the midst of tumultuous events in these last days, this book breaks open this subject that few authors have addressed. Haavard clearly defines the passion, beauty, character, glory, anointing, power, and destiny of the end-time Church—the bridal generation that will fulfill God's prophetic agenda in the last days. This book is a "beachhead" in this subject and a must read for everyone who has a passion for God's Kingdom and purposes to be fulfilled in this age and the age to come.

Bishop Daniel A. Balais
National Chairman, Intercessors for the Philippines

If you desire a deep and intimate walk with Christ, this book is for you. It takes you on a biblical adventure revealing truths and insights about the next "bridal generation." While on this journey, you will discover in-depth revelation about what passionate love is all about. It is this profound and incisive love that will usher in Christ's return for His Bride.

Peter M. Kairuz
EVP and COO of CBN ASIA, Host of 700 Club-Asia

I highly endorse the new book of Haavard called *Becoming the Bride of Christ in the Last Days*. It is about time we speak to this next generation about destiny, family, and militancy. Read it and understand. Read it and identify. Read it and be moved to believe that God is raising up a fresh, new generation madly in love with Him.

Jerome Ocampo
Director, Jesus Revolution-Philippines

Becoming the Bride of Christ in the Last Days is a must read book! For those who are hungry for more of God, this book reveals a significant portion of what He is doing in His Church at this present time. This book unravels the mystery of bridal intimacy with the lover of our soul. Let the pages of this book ignite the passion in your heart to burn for Jesus. The Spirit and the Bride say, "Come!"

Bishop Augusto "Chito" Sanchez, Jr.
Overseer, River of God Inc.
Transformation and Revival
Philippine Council of Evangelical Churches

As tidal waters pound the beach and reach farther and farther inland, the past century has seen constant new movements in the Church. Haavard Sand describes perhaps the last great movement in the age of the Church—the preparation of the Bride of Christ. Does this mean that the Bridegroom will soon return to claim His Bride?

This book has been a great source of inspiration, encouragement, and happiness. It is beautifully written and prepares the heart for an intimate encounter with Jesus. We warmly recommend this book to anyone who desires a closer relationship with Jesus, and a broader perspective of what lies ahead—in the present, as well as in eternity. This is a very important book for our time and age.

Kari and Øyvind Hofstad
Founders of the Family Ministry of
Youth With A Mission, Norway

Does your heart yearn for a deeper and more intimate relationship with Jesus? He wants one with you, too. *Becoming the Bride of Christ in the Last Days* shows us how our pursuit of true intimacy with Jesus can and will transform the world. This book will "kingdomize" your life and invite you to be part of the 21st century slugfest going on in the world. People from every nation and tongue will be a part of the Bride. The bridal generation says, YES! Your adventure has begun.

Leif Hetland
President and Founder of Global Mission Awareness

This book has impassioned and inspired us. It feeds the flame of our love for Jesus and calls forth from the deep a strong desire to surrender to the Bridegroom. And it inspires us to respond to the challenge of Colossians 3 verses 1 and 2, "to seek the things above."

Reading this book is like hunting for treasure, discovering one after the other along the way. This book makes the heart beat extra enthusiastically for Jesus—for all He has already done for us, and for what awaits us as His Bride. It inspires us to prepare for the great wedding in Heaven and is, without a doubt, a message for our time written in way that is both easy to understand and really inspiring. We give it our highest recommendation.

Tove and Jan Honningdal
Singers, songwriters, and worship leaders
Youth with a Mission, Norway

Just another book amongst many others? Not at all! It's about time for the release of such a book. In my opinion, this topic has been neglected for a long time. Jesus will come back—that's for sure! Perhaps He'll return much sooner then all of us expect. Haavard Sand's latest book is a wonderful help and a true encouragement to the Body of Christ worldwide in order to get ready for Jesus' return.

Walter Heidenreich
President of FCJG in Lüdenscheid (Germany)
& HELP International

Every once in a while, a new book comes along that brings a message that grips you. *Becoming the Bride of Christ in the Last Days* is one such book...this is a book I highly recommend.

Pastor Bob Lopez
National Director
Philippine Mission Association

TABLE OF CONTENTS

FOREWORD

The Bible uses many pictures to describe our relationship with God. He is the Good Shepherd. We are the sheep. He is our loving Father and we are His children.

He is our Savior and, at the same time, our brother–the firstborn among many brothers. He also calls us His friend; the list goes on.

These are precious and familiar pictures that we hold dear. We can easily identify with these images. But the Bible also uses another image. It is not so easy for us to identify with it because it is fresh revelation that the Holy Spirit is bringing. He is the Bridegroom and we are His Bride. In Song of Solomon this loving relationship is expressed in an understandable and direct manner. This image of the relationship between Christ and His Church can be challenging for us to relate to because it requires a great deal of intimacy and emotion that our Christian tradition finds almost inappropriate.

In the course of the first twenty-five years of my Christian life, I cannot recall hearing a message on this theme. The fact that Jesus is the Bridegroom and we are His Bride has often been mentioned in the Bible. But most teachers, myself included, have neglected to proclaim the personal richness and intimacy that are found in this image. Song of Solomon has been, for many believers, a book that is often neglected. Some may not even be sure if it belongs in the Bible at all.

In recent years, many books have been written on this topic. It seems that the Holy Spirit has begun to bring this theme and started to unveil these truths about the Bride more clearly. For it is only when the wedding approaches that the bride begins to prepare herself.

Haavard Sand goes deep into this biblical understanding. This requires a change in our mindset, our priorities, and our lifestyle. The time for the grand wedding feast is drawing near. He challenges us to prepare ourselves for that day. Jesus is coming soon to take His Bride. Time is short. The Bride must prepare herself. We must become a true bridal generation for Him to come.

In this book that is born out of loss and pain, Haavard shares openly from his personal life and experiences. He burns to share this message. This is a book that will challenge you and perhaps will make you a bit uncomfortable. But if, after you read it, you find yourself longing for a deeper love relationship with Jesus, the purpose of this book will have been achieved.

Eivind Frøen
Founder of Youth With A Mission, Norway

PREFACE

There are two main themes flowing through the Scriptures depicting our relationship with the Godhead. The first is our position as children of God, and the second is our position as the Bride of Christ. There has been much teaching that was released by the Holy Spirit, which gave understanding to us as children of God and God as the Father. This laid a foundation for the other position we have: the Church as the Bride and Jesus as the Bridegroom.

Now, the Holy Spirit is highlighting our position as the Bride to prepare the Church for the coming of the Lord. Revelation 22:17 implies that our main identity as the Church before Jesus returns is as a Bride. So, I believe the most appropriate description for the generation waiting for Jesus to return is the *bridal generation*.

This book is an attempt to give some understanding on this paradigm shift that is still new for many. These messages are just introductory, and each chapter could have been a book in itself. In many of the chapters, I have leaned heavily on different authors. My point is not only to share what has become a personal experience but to inform you about some of the things God is doing in this hour.

If you were to ask, "How long did it take to write this book," I would say fifteen years, even though much of it was written down only last year. I do not consider myself to be a writer or a prophet. If you need to give me a title, I would like to be called a treasure hunter, and this book contains the treasures I have found and collected over the years.

Some of these messages I received in seed form in the 1990s. I shared some of them during short talks at small gatherings. At that time each was like a seed, which fell to the ground, and it is only now that they are coming forth in fullness.

Some of the insights I share may come across as new to many readers. If so, I would suggest you ask two important questions: Why have I not heard this before? Why am I hearing it now?

It is not that these truths and insights are new in Scripture. They have been there all the time. But the reason why we have not grasped them before is that it has not yet been the proper time for the Holy Spirit to reveal them clearly. They seem to have been concealed until this time. As we read in the Book of Daniel, "...Go your way, Daniel, because the words are closed up and sealed until the time of the end" (Dan. 12:9). The fact that the Holy Spirit is starting to emphasize these truths these days means that the time has come for them to be fully revealed.

So who am I to write about such things? Or even suggest that I have received insights regarding what has been concealed through the ages? If this is the time for the message to be revealed, it is there for anyone who wants to press in and take hold of it. Bob Jones, a respected prophetic voice, gave this word back in 2004, "There is an awesome anointing being released at this time to write and impart to people through prophetic writing and teaching."[1]

So dear reader, if this book in any way blesses you, and you receive something from Heaven, the good news is that at this time I believe there is an open Heaven for all who hunger to receive spiritual truths and insights, to press on and take hold of them. I pray that this book will inspire you in your own search for spiritual treasures.

At the end of each chapter I have included "Questions for Reflection," which will help the reader to process what has been read. These will also be useful in small group discussions.

ENDNOTE

1. Bob Jones, quoted by Ryan Wyatt in *"Moving From Spiritual Babes To Mature Heirs"*, http://www.etpv.org/2004/mfsb2. html; accessed 20 January 2009.

PART I

Restoring the First Commandment

Restoring the first commandment is one of the most important issues, if not the most important issue, facing the Church today. In the Book of Mark, we read of Jesus being asked by one of the teachers of the law, "Of all the commandments, which is the most important?" (Mark 12:28). Jesus answers:

> *"Love the Lord your God with all your heart and with all your soul and with all your mind and with all your strength. The second is this: Love your neighbor as yourself. There is no commandment greater than these"* (Mark 12:30-31).

Jesus is telling us that loving God is the most important and the greatest commandment. But is this really the most important focus of our lives and churches? And what does living out the most important and greatest commandment really mean?

Do we fulfill the first commandment—loving God, by doing the second—loving others? Or is it by doing things for God that we fulfill the

19

first commandment? Or is living out the first commandment first of all a condition of the heart? If so, how then do we enter this reality?

These are some of the questions we will try to deal with in different ways in part I. It may not always be explicit, but restoring the first commandment is the underlying theme that will also enhance our understanding of the bridal paradigm.

Chapter 1

THE BRIDAL TRANSFORMATION— UNDERSTANDING THE TIMES

The bridal transformation that is about to happen in the Church can be described as nothing less than a revolution. The changes will be that drastic and dramatic.

The changes can be compared to that of any woman who is about to marry, and then starts to realize that her wedding day is drawing close. She will go through a process of change or transformation much like that of a caterpillar suddenly being transformed into a beautiful butterfly. That season of change is scary because in that season the caterpillar will leave her secure, small place of comfort. The temptation to stay in the cocoon will be quite strong. However, there is no turning back, and as she fights her way out of the cocoon, her wings are made strong. Finally she comes out of the cocoon, and she will be free to soar as a beautiful butterfly. People will then see her in her true identity. Before that she was just concealed in this gray unnoticeable cocoon. But now she is soaring in all her beauty, and people are pointing to her, saying, "Oh, isn't she beautiful! We did not know that all this beauty was in that cocoon. She has been utterly transformed."

Becoming the Bride of Christ in the Last Days

Going back to the analogy of the soon-to-be-wed woman, the change will first take place in her mind. Her thoughts in the past were about many things. But suddenly she becomes focused and realizes that her wedding day is soon at hand. All her attention is directed toward the wedding. All her overwhelming concerns point toward preparation for that great day. Her main preparation centers on herself: how she will look, and what she will wear.

As she continues with the preparation, the changes that take place in her mind will soon be reflected in her appearance as well. She may go to the beauty salon to try on different makeup and see which hairstyle suits her best. Perhaps she even goes on a diet and exercises to lose weight. And if her skin is pale, she might go to a tanning salon to get a tan. She will also be mindful of her wedding gown and accessories. They should look beautiful and perfect. Never before has she spent so much time on preparation for one dress—even if it is only to be worn for one day, and then stored away for safekeeping, probably never to be used again.

But then this is no ordinary day. This is her wedding day! This is the day when she is transformed into a bride. As the day approaches, she completes the last preparations and puts on her beautiful wedding dress that suddenly transforms her from being an ordinary woman into a *bride*.

When she gets to the church and is led by her father to be handed over to her bridegroom, something interesting happens. The music starts to play, the doors open, and she starts walking down the aisle with a glow on her face. Everyone is excited to see her. As she walks, all eyes are on her, and the crowd sighs as they gaze upon her because suddenly she is not just the girl next-door. No, she has become a bride.

What happens to her is what has happened to women through the ages, who have experienced being made a bride on one of the greatest days of their lives. I believe that this is also what is about to happen in the Church, which I call the *bridal transformation*.

There is a short time frame in the lives of many women who are about to marry. From being her father's daughter to becoming her husband's wife–this is a woman's special time. It's an in-between time, between two periods; it is a transition from living under her father's household to establishing a household on her own with her husband. During this short season of wedding preparation, she is no longer presented as the daughter of so-and-so, but she will only be presented as the bride.

This is the season we are about to enter into as the Church. This could be the Church's finest hour. Never before in the history of the Church have we experienced the *bridal season*, since this is the exclusive time just before the wedding.

We have been His Bride-to-be, His fiancée. It says in Second Corinthians 11:2, "I promised you to one husband, to Christ." In the Norwegian translation, this verse uses the word *engaged* or *betrothed*. Here Paul is saying that God has done this with the Church–betrothed her to Christ–but she is not yet the Bride. If you are a man engaged to be married in six months' time, your future wife is not yet called a bride, but your fiancée. At a certain time just before the wedding, she goes from being your fiancée to becoming the bride. And later, she becomes your wife.

The last revelation of the Church in the Bible is as the Bride. It is only when we turn to the last pages of the Bible that Scripture clearly talks about the Church as the Bride. It is only at the end of time, just before the Second Coming, that the Church is described as the Bride. Scripture tells us, "The Spirit and the bride say, 'Come!'" (Rev. 22:17). This means it will be a time before the end when Jesus has not yet come back.

Then the Church will have reached her bridal season. The very fact that this has not really been a part of Church identity through the ages is proof in itself that the bridal season has not yet arrived. However, Scripture tells us that this time will come, and we may soon start seeing the first signs of this occurrence. You don't need to tell a bride that she is a bride! She knows it. It influences her whole being. And one day soon, the Church will enter the bridal season. Then she will know she is the Bride.

So the generation that will experience this, which I call the bridal generation, will experience something unprecedented in Church history that none of the saints of old have experienced—the bridal season.

We may like to imagine how it would have been to live in the time of Jesus. Naturally, that was a unique time, but I believe that some of the disciples, if they could choose, might have chosen our time—the days of the bridal generation.

A CHOSEN GENERATION

Through Scripture we learn that some generations are chosen over others in a special way—to see and experience the glory of God in a special time of transition.

Moses' generation was one such generation. For hundreds of years, the Israelites had lived as slaves under Pharaoh. Day in and day out they had to cope with hard labor. No interventions from God. One year came and another year went. This continued for about four hundred years. Then suddenly, at a special time in history God intervened. One chosen generation was allowed to witness His mighty deliverance and experienced the transition from a life in slavery to the joy of freedom.

Something similar happened again at the time of Jesus. For about four hundred years, the heavens were silent, and no great intervention or act of God was seen. But suddenly, one generation was chosen among the others. To be the generation to witness how God became flesh—dwelling among men—that certainly was one of the greatest privileges ever given to any generation.

However, only one generation is chosen to experience the bridal season on earth. To walk those last steps before the Bride meets her Bridegroom, for all men to see and marvel at her beauty. And as she crosses the line into eternity she joins with the saints of old, the ones gone before her. In Hebrews, we read:

These were all commended for their faith, yet none of them received what had been promised. God had planned something better for us so that only together with us would they be made perfect (Hebrews 11:39-40).

I believe this Scripture will be fulfilled as we see it happen in history, at the end of the age. It is in fellowship with all the saints from the ages—completing the race all the way to the end—that together we may be made perfect and receive "what had been promised."

Then the author of Hebrews goes on to exhort us to run the race and free ourselves from everything that hinders, as we are surrounded by this great cloud of witnesses (see Heb. 12:1). The saints of old should be our inspiration to press on.

How then is this great cloud of witnesses supposed to be an inspiration for us to carry on? First, we can study their lives, and learn how they became witnesses during their time, and how they can inspire us in running our race. Second, we can find strength in them as we imagine that they too are witnessing our lives, cheering us on. This assurance should bring us the strength we need to endure our own race.

The ultimate reason they are cheering us on, is that they know that without us they will not be made perfect, for we really belong to each other. Together, we with the saints of old will once be made perfect and be made into the Bride of Christ. This is the ultimate goal: "to present her to Himself as a radiant church, without stain or wrinkle or any other blemish, but holy and blameless" (Eph. 5:27).

Ephesians 5:27 is the fulfillment of Hebrews 11:39-40. That we together with them will be made perfect as the Bride of Christ. What then was the promise they still have not received? (See Hebrews 11:39-40.) Was it different from the promise Jesus looked forward to? Hebrews teaches us how Jesus "for the joy set before Him endured the cross" (Heb. 12:2). What was the joy or promise set before Him—other than the Bride? Jesus calls Himself the Bridegroom (see Matt. 9:15). What is the joy set before the Bridegroom—other than His Bride on their wedding day? The only time God defines His joy is in Isaiah:

As a young man marries a maiden, so will your sons marry you; as a bridegroom rejoices over his bride, so will your God rejoice over you (Isaiah 62:5).

Here God is saying, "Do you want to know what My joy is like? It is like a bridegroom rejoicing over his bride!" So if that is how His joy is defined, then that would certainly be the joy set before Him— His Bride! Likewise, the joy and the promise set before the Bride is her Bridegroom on their wedding day.

That is why there is a special connection between the bridal generation and the great cloud of witnesses. For these witnesses know that when the bridal generation crosses the line, then we will all be made perfect and receive this promise together.

The bridal generation will be the generation that crosses the line from one dispensation to another. They will do it as the Bride never seeing death. Our last enemy is death, but this generation will never meet it. They will meet instead their Bridegroom who is life. Isn't that an incredible thought? If we are that generation, we will never face death but just be changed from a temporal life to eternal life.

A New Expression of Christianity

Mike Bickle shares about this change that is coming to the Church, based on a supernatural encounter he had in a hotel room in Cairo, Egypt, in September 1982. He writes:

> I didn't see a vision, and I wasn't caught up into heaven. I simply heard God speak to me. It wasn't what some people call the audible voice. I call it the internal audible voice. I heard it as clearly as I would have heard it with my physical ears and, honestly, it was terrifying.

> It came with such a feeling of cleanness, power and authority. In some ways, I felt I was being crushed by it. I wanted to leave, but I didn't want to leave. I wanted it to be over, but I didn't want it to be over. I only heard a few sentences, and it took just a few moments, but every word had great meaning. The awe of God flooded my soul as I experienced a little bit of the terror of the Lord. I literally trembled and

wept as God Himself communicated to me in a way I've never known before or since. The Lord simply said, "I will change the understanding and expression of Christianity in the earth in one generation." It was a simple, straightforward statement, but I felt God's power with each word as I received the Spirit's interpretation.

I understood that this reformation/revival would be His sovereign initiative. God Himself was going to make this drastic change in Christianity across the world. The phrase "the understanding of Christianity" meant the way Christianity is perceived by unbelievers. In the early church people were afraid to associate even casually with believers partly because of the displays of supernatural power. In the 1990s most unbelievers consider the church to be irrelevant.

God will change the way unbelievers view the church. They once again will witness God's wonderful yet terrifying power in the church. They will have a different understanding of Christianity before God is finished with this generation.

The phrase "expression of Christianity" meant the way the body of Christ expresses its life together. God is powerfully going to change the church so that it functions effectively as a healthy body in the power and love of God instead of just having meetings and programs based on its design and structure.

Paul Cain says that there are three elements of this new understanding and expression: unparalleled power, purity and unity. Christians' relationship with God and with each other, the way they are perceived by unbelievers, and even the structure and functioning of the church will be radically and suddenly changed by God Himself.

And this change will take place—not in a month, a year or a few years—but in one generation. That night in Cairo I had the sense that I was being invited to be part of this...Above all things, it will impart and renew deep, affectionate passion for Jesus by the Holy Spirit. The Holy Spirit longs above all things to glorify Jesus in the human heart (John 16:14). He wants to impart deep and holy affection for Jesus in the Bride of Christ.[1]

This will be the bridal generation that will arise and shine in unparalleled power, purity (regarding her beauty), and unity (regarding her being one Bride). After all, Jesus is coming back for one Bride, which is one of the main reasons why unity is so important. Furthermore, I believe that pivotal to this encounter of Mike Bickle with God is the understanding of the Church of her position as the Bride of Christ, since this position is an emphasis on intimacy or deep affection.

And as the Bride will arise and shine, the world will look in amazement because of her emanating beauty and undeniable power that has become irresistible. Then many will turn and become part of the Bride themselves, as she marches the last walk down the aisle before she meets Him.

THE UNVEILING OF THE BRIDE

As you read this interpretation you may say, "Well, you are using the illustration from a Western wedding, but that is very different from a Jewish wedding, which was the cultural setting Jesus was talking and living in." Yes, but this is greater than any Jewish wedding. This is the wedding of all ages. We need all the wedding traditions of the world to give us an understanding of what is coming, and even that will still not be sufficient.

Certainly, the primary way a wedding is pictured and understood today—the Western tradition, which has become universal through the movie industry—is not there by chance. I think it was prophetically given by the Lord to give us a clear prophetic image of what is about to happen to the Church.

In Western tradition, there is a stage before the bride meets with her bridegroom where both guests and spectators get to see the bride. This happens as the bride is ushered down the aisle by her father. For that brief moment, the bride is presented for everyone to see.

This is a picture of what happens when the Holy Spirit escorts the Church to be handed over to the Bridegroom. We are approaching that day when the Bride will be ready and be led by the Spirit. Then the Bride will be shown in all her power and beauty for all the world to see. As she marches that last walk down the aisle of this world–telling the Good News of the King and His everlasting Kingdom, proclaiming and demonstrating its power–multitudes will join her and become the Bride themselves.

Deep within the Bridegroom's heart is this longing to display His Bride in all her beauty. When that day finally comes, the world will marvel at what it sees. In his book, *Bridal Intercession,* Gary Wiens touches on the subject of God showing all people His Bride:

> Throughout the Scripture, the people of God are seen as the primary vehicle for the exhibition of His glory. In Isaiah 62:3 we are told that God will hold His people as a crown of glory in His hand, with the express purpose of exhibiting their beauty as a testimony of His power and grace.

> First Corinthians 11 declares that the glory of a man is his wife, and that man is "the glory of God."

> Furthermore, according to Ephesians 3:10, a day is coming when through the Church of Jesus Christ the wisdom and glory of God will be manifested to the principalities and powers in the heavenly places. In other words, God is going to exhibit the beauty and glory of His Bride, the Church, and the spiritual powers in heavenly places will fall down before the Bride and before her King, declaring His glory and power as His wisdom is vindicated for all to see.

What a picture of grace: the King of kings, exhibiting His matchless glory, as revealed through His Bride, the redeemed and sanctified Church![2]

Just as this will be shown before the spiritual powers in the heavenly realm, it will also be done for all the earth to see. The Bridegroom of all bridegrooms is going to show forth His Bride. As Wiens states, First Corinthians 11:7 says that man is His glory, just as "woman is the glory of man."

This will be part of the fulfillment of Habakkuk: "For the earth will be filled with the knowledge of the glory of the Lord, as the waters cover the sea" (Hab. 2:14). If part of the glory of the Lord is His Bride, as we have seen, then this Scripture tells us that at one point, the world will be filled with the knowledge of the Bride, as the waters cover the sea!

I don't know how long this walk down the aisle on the world will last. But I am sure of one thing: it will be longer than one day of our calendar, because the Lord is operating with a different calendar.

Then, as the Bride approaches the altar, the scene shifts. We now find the Spirit and the Bride crying together, "Come!" (see Rev. 22:17). And as this cry reaches a crescendo in the Father's appointed time, the heavens will break, and Jesus will come for His Bride. Scripture is very clear that the revelation of the Church at the end of the age will be as the Bride. As it says in Revelation, "His bride has made herself ready" (Rev. 19:7). When does a bride make herself ready? Before the wedding. When she meets her bridegroom, she is already ready. She wants to show her very best side to him on the day of their wedding.

This change of understanding is coming with the bridal generation. Through all Church history, the teaching about getting ready to meet the Lord has been focused on self—making sure I will make it, that I am clean and ready, so that I can make it to Heaven. This has naturally been a very foundational and important message.

However, as the bridal generation arises, the understanding and focus of what it means to make oneself ready will shift. The Church's primary focus will be the preparation of herself. The Bride will not just concentrate on making sure that she makes it to her wedding day; she has already set that day apart a long time ago, when she said yes to Him. What is now foremost on her mind, as she prepares herself for that day, is that she wants to look her very best for Him.

And as she enters the heavens, she is given a bright and clean dress to wear, symbolizing the righteous acts of the saints (see Rev. 19:8). She will receive a heavenly dress, which is the product of her righteous acts. So Scripture is clear, the world will see her wearing her wedding dress through her righteous acts. And it will be the acts of the apostles all over again—and more.

Now, let us consider what it says in Romans chapter 8:

> *The creation waits in eager expectation for the sons of God to be revealed...We know that the whole creation has been groaning as in pains of childbirth right up to the present time* (Romans 8:19,22).

The whole creation is waiting; it is groaning and longing for the day when we will be revealed as "the sons of God" (Rom. 8:19). It is like the whole creation waits for the Church to reach her maturity as sons of God, which is our position before the Father. As we stand before the Son, we are His coming Bride. And if we apply this Scripture as relating to our position before the Son, it would mean something like this: the creation waits in eager expectation for the *Bride of Christ* to be revealed!

Friends, do you believe that the entire creation—in fact, the whole universe—is waiting, groaning, and longing for that day when the Bride will be revealed? Could it be that this awesome privilege has been given to us, and we are in fact the bridal generation, which is soon to arise on earth?

ENDNOTES

1. Mike Bickle, *Growing in the Prophetic* (Orlando, FL: Creation House, 1996), 29-31.

2. Gary Wiens, *Bridal Intercession* (Greenwood, MO: Oasis House, 2001), 86.

Questions for Reflection

1. Do you see evidence of what God is doing in churches today that indicates we are entering the bridal season? If so, what are some of these indications? How can you become part of this season?

2. What is the focus of your life today? Are your eyes fixed on the Bridegroom; are you finding your destiny in Him?

Chapter 2

THE CAPTURED HEART—BECOMING BEAUTY SEEKERS

Beauty is the battlefield where God and Satan contend with each other for the hearts of men.

from *The Brothers Karamazov*
by Fyodor Dostoyevsky

THE PURSUIT OF THE BRIDAL GENERATION

Why did Jesus come? To save us, to cleanse us from our sins and give us everlasting life! But what compelled Him to do that? He came because He loved us. But I want to be even more specific than that: He came because His heart was captured by you and me, His Bride-to-be. Song of Solomon says, "You have captured my heart, my treasure, my bride" (Song of Sol. 4:9 NLT).

Jesus came because His heart was *captured* by you and me. This is truly the story of the prince in his shining armor who came to rescue and save his bride-to-be from the dragon of old. And as Jesus came and fought the ultimate fight for love, to kill that dragon and set His princess free, He died in the battle. He died in the battle of the ages. He died in the battle for His Bride. He died for love, and He died in love.

As He was gasping for breath, His last words—according to John—were "it is finished" (John 19:30). When He was hanging there on that cross in incredible pain, His last thought was about you and me. In Hebrew, the word *finished* is *kalah*, the same word from which the word *bride* is taken.

So when Jesus said it is "finished," He was saying "bride" at the same time. He was saying this so that it would ring true in all of history. "My Bride, it is finished. I saved you and rescued you from the dragon of old. I did it all because My heart was captured by you."

You see, that is our Prince; He did it all because we captured His heart. And now His question for you and me is, "As My heart was captured by you, is your heart captured by Me?" That is really what He is seeking; He is looking for hearts that have been captured by Him.

Imagine if the one you were planning to marry promised to give you all that you wanted: a big house with a large garden, a nice car, beautiful children, and unlimited shopping privileges. But then imagine he told you that he would give you everything except one thing. Maybe you would think, *If I get all these things, I can always manage not having that one thing he can't give.* Then imagine asking him, "What is that one thing you can't give me," and hearing him answer, "The thing I can't give you and never will is—my heart."

How could you then proceed with the marriage? There are those who marry for money, but their marriages usually end miserably. For if the heart is not in it, how can you go through with it? Isn't marriage about giving one's heart?

It is the heart that Jesus is after because he is a lover, and a lover always seeks the heart. What's the first and greatest commandment?

Jesus replied: "'Love the Lord your God with all your heart and with all your soul and with all your mind.' This is the first and greatest commandment. And the second is like it: 'Love your neighbor as yourself. All the Law and the Prophets hang on these two command-ments" (Matthew 22:37-40).

This is our ultimate call, and it can be fulfilled if we follow what it says in the first phrase—to "love the Lord your God with all your heart." In that one statement, I believe it is all fulfilled because who can love anyone if it is not from the heart? In his book, *Waking the Dead,* John Eldredge shares this insight from the famous story of the yellow brick road.

> On her journey down the yellow brick road—a jour-ney, may I remind you, that grows more dangerous every step she takes, Dorothy meets a number of strange sights. She befriends the Scarecrow, and later the two of them come upon a lumberjack made of tin, standing utterly still in the forest, his ax frozen in midair. At first, he seems unable to speak. Com-ing closer, they discover that he is trying to say something after all. "Oil…can." After a bit more mis-understanding and misinterpretation, they get the oilcan to the joints of his mouth, only to find that he can speak as well as any man, but that he was rusted. Once he is freed from his prison, he begins to tell them his story.[1]

The tin woodman in the fairy tale had once been a real man who had been in love with a beautiful maiden. He longed to marry her, but the wicked witch hated his love for the maiden. So she cast spells upon the man that caused him injury. One by one his limbs needed to be replaced with artificial ones made of tin. At first, he thought it was to his advantage to have a metal frame, which allowed him to work nearly as powerfully as a machine. With a heart of love and arms that never tired, he seemed sure to win. As L. Frank Baum writes of the tin woodman in *The Wonderful Wizard of Oz:*

> I thought I had beaten the Wicked Witch then, and I worked harder than ever; but I little knew how cruel my enemy could be. She thought of a new way to kill my love for the beautiful Munchkin maiden,

and made my axe slip again, so that it cut right through my body, splitting it into two halves. Once more the tinner came to my help and made me a body of tin. Fastening my tin arms and legs and head to it, by means of joints, so that I could move around as well as ever. But alas! I now had no heart, so that I lost all my love for the Munchkin girl, and did not care whether I married her or not....

My body shone so brightly in the sun that I felt very proud of it and it did not matter now if my axe slipped, for it could not cut me, There was only one danger—that my joints would rust; but I kept an oil-can in the cottage and took care to oil myself whenever I needed it. However, there came a day when I forgot to do this, and being caught in a rainstorm, before I had thought of the danger my joints had rusted, and I was left to stand in the woods until you came to help me.

It was a terrible thing to undergo, but during the year I stood there I had time to think that the greatest loss I had known was the loss of my heart. While I was in love I was the happiest man on earth; but no one can love who has not a heart.[2]

It's all about the heart, and there is one who—like the wicked witch—hates our love for the Lord, and who will do anything to cut us off from living from the heart. For only by living from the heart are we able to love. "Above all else, guard your heart, for it is the wellspring of life" (Prov. 4:23).

It is from our heart that life flows, as does our ability to love. And as we love Him with all our heart, we will then eventually love Him with all our soul, mind, and strength. But it all flows from the heart.

If this is true, what does it mean then to love Him with all our heart? That should be our single most important question because this is our highest calling. It is what Jesus said was the most important thing to do (see Mark 12:28-31). So then how do we fulfill the great commandment? Only the heart that is captured by God can fulfill the great commandment. To love the Lord your God with all your heart is not at all just about doing things for Him. It certainly goes far beyond that. The Pharisees zealously did all the right things for God, but Jesus still rebuked them. He said:

> *...Isaiah was right when he prophesied about you: "These people honor Me with their lips, but their hearts are far from Me. They worship Me in vain; their teachings are but rules taught by men"* (Matthew 15:7-9).

What was their problem? They did many things, but their actions did not flow from a captured heart—so loving God can't be about following rules and regulations.

So often our testimony is about trying our best to follow the Lord, about living a life focused on rules and regulations. Friends, that is not Christianity. That is not the life the Lord has called us to. That is religion and that is death because it does not have life in it. It is not a life lived from the heart.

Christianity is not about trying to be good and living a respectable life. It is not even about trying to get a ticket to Heaven. It is instead about having our hearts captured by Him because this is our love story.

Sometimes our thrust in evangelism is about praying a simple prayer so that one can be blessed by God and go to Heaven after one dies. Next we say, "Here are some rules and regulations you now have to follow as a believer. Try your best and confess your sins and then you will be blessed and go to Heaven when you die." Many believers are hanging onto this understanding—trying their best on their way to Heaven. But their hearts are never captured. The truth is that this misunderstanding has a lot to do with the way we have presented the Gospel. People have said yes and received Christ with the focus on what they could get out of it.

But we have and are part of the most amazing love story ever told—about the most beautiful Prince who ever lived, and the most extravagant love ever displayed. Let's share this with passion so that people's hearts can be captured.

CAPTURED BY BEAUTY

The big question arises, "What is it that captures the heart?" Simone Weil writes, "There are only two things that pierce the human heart, one is beauty; the other is affliction." Beauty has the ability to pierce or capture the human heart.

> Beauty has a universal reach. No human is immune from the magnetic appeal of whatever he/she regards as beautiful. In *The Brothers Karamazov*, Fyodor Dostoyevsky placed on the lips of one of his characters the observation that "beauty is the battlefield where God and Satan contend with each other for the hearts of men."[3]

You see our hearts are created in such a way that they long to be captured, thrilled, and fascinated by beauty. We don't need to force ourselves to be captured by beauty. It comes naturally; it is the way we are made.

Take a look at a woman entering a beautiful home. She does not have to walk around trying to cultivate some kind of excitement over what she sees. She is captured. Effortlessly, she is naturally enamored. She says, "Wow! This is so beautiful!" She is thrilled and fascinated. And when she enters the bathroom with all the small perfume bottles, beautiful tiles, and decorations she is totally lost. She is captured, and it did not cost her one ounce of hard work.

We are naturally attracted to beauty. But the world perverts it so that we settle for what Sam Storms calls "lesser beauties". To add what C.S. Lewis said, "The problem with this generation is that they are too easily satisfied." Therefore, we are misled and deceived, and we land on inferior beauties. How do we avoid this tendency so we can live with a heart that is captured and fascinated without going astray? We resolve to fix our gaze on Jesus who is the One of ultimate beauty.

We were created to be captured, thrilled, and fascinated by beauty. *And Jesus, our Prince, who created everything beautiful, is the One of ultimate beauty.* As noted theologian Hans Urs Von Balthasar has said, "Every experience of beauty points us to infinity." In other words, every experience of beauty points us to God.

David's heart was captured by God. He came to the point where gazing upon God's beauty was his highest goal in life. As he wrote in Psalms:

> *One thing I ask of the Lord, this is what I seek: that I may dwell in the house of the Lord all the days of my life, to gaze upon the beauty of the Lord and to seek Him in His temple* (Psalm 27:4).

David was a busy man, the ruler of a large kingdom. Being a king in a palace, he was also surrounded by many lesser beauties. But he didn't let any of them hinder him from gazing at the One of ultimate beauty. He was a man who sought to gaze upon the beauty of God above all things.

This was also the one thing Mary—who sat at the feet of Jesus—had chosen. Jesus said that she had chosen what was better, and that it would not be taken away from her (see Luke 10:42).

As we read on in Psalm 27, we see what has happened with David. He says, "My heart says of You, 'Seek His face!' Your face, Lord, I will seek" (Ps. 27:8). Here we see that his heart has come alive. It now speaks. Why? Because it has been captured by beauty. The heart that has been captured and has seen the One of ultimate beauty now longs for more. It knows the very place to find it—the face of Jesus, the face being the focal point of a person's beauty. The heart says, "I want to have a face-to-face experience. I want to gaze at the very beauty of His face."

It says in Second Corinthians:

> *For God, who said, "Let light shine out of darkness," made His light shine in our hearts to give us the light of the knowledge of the glory of God in the face of Christ* (2 Corinthians 4:6).

God lets His light shine in our hearts so we can be captured by the knowledge of the glory of God's beauty, which is found in the face of Jesus. Throughout the Bible, we are encouraged time and again to seek His face, to allow our hearts to be captured by His beauty afresh. We are encouraged to seek His face in Second Chronicles:

> *If My people, who are called by My name, will humble themselves and pray and seek My face and turn from their wicked ways, then will I hear from heaven and will forgive their sin and will heal their land* (2 Chronicles 7:14).

After we humble ourselves and pray, we are encouraged to seek His face. We are told to turn back from where we have fallen, from where we have lost sight of His beauty, and from where we have been captured by lesser beauties. David again and again returned to the face of God. He wrote, "Let the light of Your face shine upon us, O Lord" (Ps. 4:6).

The blessing recorded in Numbers says:

> *The Lord bless you and keep you; the Lord make His face shine upon you and be gracious to you; the Lord turn His face toward you and give you peace* (Numbers 6:24-26).

Here *face* is mentioned twice; we need the beauty of His face to shine upon us.

THE BEAUTY OF GOD IN CREATION

What do we gaze at to look on the beauty of God? We do this by looking at God's three books that reflect His beauty. He has one ultimate book, the Bible that contains the canon of Scripture, which is the infallible and unfading means that reveals His beauty. However, there are two other books that I believe we can look at to see His beauty. First is creation. He created this for us to enjoy it and be thrilled by it. David contemplating God's beauty said:

> *The heavens declare the glory of God; the skies proclaim the work of His hands. Day after day they pour forth speech; night after night*

they display knowledge. There is no speech or language where their voice is not heard. Their voice goes out into all the earth, their words to the ends of the world...(Psalm 19:1-4).

It says that the heavens declare the glory (or beauty) of God, and the skies proclaim the work of His hands, and it continues to say that this proclaiming goes on night and day. This language of beauty in creation is universally understood.

Creation is awesome. We need to allow our hearts to be captured by the beauty of creation again. Not that we should worship creation, but that it should lead us to worship the Creator even more.

We all have this "wow" inside of us. When someone comes to you and shows you something beautiful they have made, what is your normal reaction? Probably something like, "Wow, that is beautiful!" But you don't start to worship what they made, right? No, you praise the maker.

Think of a time when you have experienced nature, looking at some of the beauty of God's creation. Now consider, when was the last time you said, "Wow, God, that is beautiful!" He is an incredible God! It is time we rouse the "wow" we have inside of us and burst out some big wows to God for the beauty of His creation.

So let me just give you a few starters to awaken you. Let's start with animals and plants. It is estimated that there are up to 10 million different species of them. That's an incredible number, and each one is unique—with the most intricate and breathtaking design.

Looking at the animal kingdom, we may note that each animal appears on earth perfect, according to its kind. That fact alone should make the followers of Darwin's theory ask themselves some serious questions. No geological records of partially adapted species exist so far. Nor are there any awkward transitional forms on earth today. Each animal is perfect, according to its kind.

Let's then look at how perfect they are. A bird, for example. Let's read how Thomas Dubay describes a bird:

Everything about a bird is elegant almost beyond belief: the pneumatic skeleton, extremely light with its air-filled hollows and yet extraordinarily strong; air sacs throughout the body, which provide air circulation that cools the bird like a radiator; the enormous expenditure of energy needed to sustain the hyperactivity of flight, which in turn demands not only the highly efficient cooling system, but also an immense consummation of food for fuel; the intricate design of feathers and wings of diverse types for differing functions; the marvelous motions of wings so ingenious that engineers study them to learn how to solve problems in designing aircraft that can ascend, descend, take off, and land, moving from left to right and right to left.[4]

Then if we zero in on just one kind of bird, like the eagle, we find that they are so skilled in flying that they can dive at 300 kilometers per hour without any problems. And among eagles alone we find 59 known species!

Now let's look at flowers. Imagine flowers, how each one is unique and breathtakingly beautiful. But because there are so many of them we have taken them for granted, and they have lost their ability to awe us. Imagine if one orchid were the only flower that existed in the world. If that orchid were displayed in an exhibit at the greatest museums of the world, you could be sure that thousands upon thousands of people would line up for hours just to take a look at its beauty and smell its fragrance.

Let's say it was a green catasetum orchid, once described like this, "Any perfumer who penetrated the secret of that scent could make a small fortune."[5] This is just one of many different kinds of orchids. Actually, it is estimated that there are approximately 35,000 of them, but just one alone could have swept us off our feet.

We finally arrive at the crown of creation, man himself. Of the many things we can say about man and his intricate and marvelous design, let's zero in on one fact alone. The Human Genome Project, which is an international scientific effort to map the entire DNA code of Homo sapiens, has concluded that the code is so great it is expected to occupy 200,000 pages of dictionary-size small print. We are truly God's work of art, "fearfully and wonderfully made" (see Ps. 139:14).[6]

Outside of man himself, let's now look at the ultimate expression of the beauty and greatness of God in creation. To experience the ultimate beauty of God in creation, take time to go out one night when the sky is clear. Lie down in an open space, and look straight to the sky. Gazing at it, you will see some of the greatness and wonder of God, which you can't find anywhere else in His creation. You are like a speck of dust compared to all you see.

While you do this, you should realize that you are looking at our galaxy, the Milky Way. There are 150–200 billion stars in our galaxy alone. Wow! Then consider that there are something like 150 billion galaxies in existence. One galaxy, called Virgo, has more than 5 trillion stars alone, and God knows them all by name (see Ps. 147:4). It is too mind-boggling to grasp!

Regarding size, the sun (which is a rather small star with a diameter of 864,000 miles) is still so large that if you put 100 earths side by side, it would still not span the diameter of the sun. Then consider one of the biggest stars in our galaxy, known as *Eta Carinae*. This star has a diameter of more than 400 million miles. That is truly huge; it is more than 400 times the size of the sun. Or consider energy: the *Pistol* star glows with an energy 10 million times that of our sun. That's hot![7]

And then imagine that as you lie there looking at the sky and allowing your heart to be captured by everything you see, the Creator looks at you and rejoices over you. Imagine Him calling His angels over and pointing down at you, saying, "Do you see one of My children has stopped from his busy schedule, just to gaze upon the beauty of My creation? I created it all for them to enjoy and to be captured by it."

I believe David loved to do this, too. In Psalms chapter 8, we find him out at night watching the starry host saying, "When I consider Your heavens, the work of Your fingers, the moon and the stars, which

You have set in place" (Ps. 8:3). His gaze at God's creation would lead him to worship. Like David, we too can be captured by the breathtaking beauty and splendor of creation and begin to worship.

Just as we see the greatness and beauty of God in macrocosmos, so is the case with microcosmos. For example, consider an atom, which is a fairly small object. It is so small that if you lined up 30 million of them, it would cover a distance of about one centimeter.

An interesting thing about an atom is that it consists mostly of empty space. In that space, we find a small particle called a nucleus. Sam Storms gives the following illustration to help us imagine how small the nucleus is compared to an atom.

> Think of an atom as if it were a typical football stadium, like the Rose Bowl in Pasadena, California. If such were an atom, the nucleus would be the size of a single grain of sand on the fifty-yard line. If it helps to put a number on it, here goes. The nucleus of an atom comprises only one part in 100,000,000,000,000, that's one part in 100 trillion! Now that's tiny![8]

Then inside the nucleus we find particles called protons and neutrons, up to 200 of them. Inside the protons and neutrons we find the quark, which is less than one-thousandth the size of a proton or neutron. This is what physicists believe to be the fundamental building block of all existing matter, and it is small.[9]

Now, remember that God fashioned and made it all–from the greatest star to the tiniest quark–in all its greatness and intricate detail. That truly deserves our biggest "Wow!"

THE BEAUTY OF GOD IN MAN'S HEART

Now, we have come to the second book we can read to be captured by the beauty of God. It is the beauty of God at work in the heart of man. When we see God at work in the heart of man–how He transforms even the lowliest person into something beautiful–we are gazing at His beauty.

We see this when He rescues a prostitute from living on the streets and selling her own body, which is completely destroyed by drugs. She comes to Him, gets off the street, regains her dignity, and is set free from addiction. She has traded the ashes of her life for beauty. When we see this, we are gazing at beauty in one of God's books.

In Second Corinthians, Paul tells us that we "are a letter from Christ...written not with ink but with the Spirit of the living God" (2 Cor. 3:3). Just as the Bible contains many letters written by the Spirit, so are we a letter written by the Spirit. As we peek into the beauty of God's work in the heart of man, we're actually reading one of Christ's letters.

Several years ago as I worked with our Discipleship Training School (DTS) at a Youth With A Mission (YWAM) base in Norway, one of our students had a very touching experience with the Lord. It was the season of renewal in the mid-1990s. We had a week of teaching about the Holy Spirit, and Peter Helms was sharing.

During one of the ministry sessions, this student was sitting on the floor laughing uncontrollably. Her actions seemed quite strange to those of us looking at it from the outside because we could not see the beauty of what God had written on her heart. By the time we were going for our break, she was still so overcome by the Spirit that she was not able to talk properly; whenever she tried to talk she could only speak in tongues.

Later, she shared what had happened to her as she was sitting there on the floor. She had always had a problem, and to you this problem may seem insignificant, but for her it was significant. As she grew up—and even after coming to the DTS—she always felt like an outsider when her friends would sit around sharing stories and cracking jokes. She felt as if no one else wanted to listen to her stories.

While she sat there on the floor, she experienced that Jesus came to her and told her He wanted to hear her stories. Then they sat sharing stories with each other and laughing. When I hear a story like that I know I am gazing on the beauty of God in the heart of man, and some more of my false perceptions of God fall to the ground. It is in these moments that I see more of His unfathomable love and care.

Perhaps, some of you who are reading may think that this is exaggerated and would say, "Jesus wouldn't come and sit and laugh and share stories with someone like that." Well, what about the Scripture that says:

> *If you, then, though you are evil, know how to give good gifts to your children, how much more will Your Father in heaven give good gifts to those who ask Him!* (Matthew 7:11)

If a daughter were to come home from school crying, what father on earth would not sit down with her to find out what the problem was? If she said that no one would listen to her, wouldn't he be the first one to say, "If no one else wants to listen, I will." And then she would tell her stories, and they would laugh together. The Bible tells us that though we are evil we give good gifts to our children. How much more will our heavenly Father do that for us?

BEAUTY OF GOD IN HIS WORD

The primary book where we can gaze on the beauty of God is, of course, the Bible. So how do we do that? First of all, we study and meditate on the life of Jesus. We look at how He went around during His earthly ministry to help anyone in need, and how He gave Himself in death on the cross. Then we will be gazing into the One of ultimate beauty, the beauty of the love of Jesus' heart.

Jesus said, "Anyone who has seen Me has seen the Father" (John 14:9). But we can even gaze on the external beauty of God, what theologians call the theophanies or the "God pictures." Although most of us have not literally seen the external beauty of God, some have. It is written down in the Bible, and I believe it is there for us to gaze at and meditate on.

Let's look at John's experience on the island of Patmos. In Revelation, he writes:

> *I turned around to see the voice that was speaking to me. And when I turned I saw seven golden lampstands, and among the lampstands was someone "like a son of man," dressed in a robe reaching down to His feet and with a golden sash around His chest. His head and hair*

were white like wool, as white as snow, and His eyes were like blazing fire. His feet were like bronze glowing in a furnace, and His voice was like the sound of rushing waters. In His right hand He held seven stars, and out of His mouth came a sharp double-edged sword. His face was like the sun shining in all its brilliance (Revelation 1:12-16).

Here John is gazing upon the One of ultimate beauty, and he does not have to try to be captured. Can you imagine what he experienced? Hollywood with all its glamour and special effects cannot match the ability of God to capture the human heart.

There are also other passages for us to read and meditate upon, which tell of people who saw God. For example, see Isaiah chapter 6, Ezekiel chapters 1 and 10, and Song of Solomon chapter 5 verses 10 through 16 (where the bride is describing the beauty of her lover). Then we have Revelation chapters 4 and 5, which Mike Bickle calls the beauty realm of God. There we can gaze not only on the beauty of God Himself, but also on the beauty of the place where He dwells.

Take these passages, read them, meditate on them, and allow your heart to be captured by the beauty of God. As we close this chapter let us again give ear to Sam Storms, as he describes the beauty of God:

> God alone is beautiful in an absolute and unqualified sense. In God alone are perfect proportion, harmony, unity, and diversity in delicate balance, stunning brilliance, and integrity. God is beautiful! If we were able to think of God as a painting, we would say that there are no random brush strokes, no clashes of colors. God is aesthetically exquisite. In God there is absolute resolution, integration, the utter absence of even one discordant element.
>
> God has, as it were, placed Himself on display in the art gallery of the universe. He beckons His people, you and me, to stand in awe as we behold the symmetry of His attributes, the harmony of His deeds, the glory of His goodness, the overwhelming and

unfathomable grandeur of His greatness; in a word, His beauty. God is infinitely splendid and invites us to come and bask in His beauty that we might enjoy Him to the fullest.[10]

ENDNOTES

1. John Eldredge, *Waking the Dead–The Glory of God Fully Alive* (Nashville, TN: Thomas Nelson, Inc., 2003), 36.

2. John Eldredge, *Waking the Dead–The Glory of God Fully Alive* (Nashville, TN: Thomas Nelson, Inc., 2003), 37-38.

3. Sam Storms, *One Thing–Developing a Passion for the Beauty of God* (Scotland, Great Britain: Christian Focus Publications Ltd., 2004), 49-50.

4. Thomas Dubay, *The Evidential Power of Beauty–Science and Theology Meet* (San Francisco, CA: Ignatius Press, 1999), 32.

5. Luis Marden, "The Exquisite Orchids," *National Geographic* (April 1971), 502.

6. Much of the information contained in the section entitled, "The Beauty of God in Creation" is adapted from Thomas Dubay, *The Evidential Power of Beauty–Science and Theology Meet*, (San Francisco, CA: Ignatius Press, 1999), 31, 33-34, 150-152.

7. The scientific information on figures about the universe was taken from Sam Storms, *One Thing–Developing a Passion for the Beauty of God*, (Scotland, Great Britain: Christian Focus Publications Ltd., 2004), 92-94.

8. Sam Storms, *One Thing–Developing a Passion for the Beauty of God* (Scotland, Great Britain: Christian Focus Publications Ltd., 2004), 111.

9. The information on microcosmos was taken from Sam Storms, *One Thing–Developing a Passion for the Beauty of God*,

(Scotland, Great Britain: Christian Focus Publications Ltd., 2004), 111-113.

10. Sam Storms, *Pleasure Evermore* (Colorado Springs, CO: NavPress, 2000), 54.

Questions for Reflection

1. What is it that naturally captures your heart?

2. How does fixing your eyes on the One of ultimate beauty inspire you to draw closer to Him everyday?

3. What is something in your heart that disables you from living from the heart? What are the things you think are necessary to prepare your heart to receive more of His presence?

Chapter 3

THE OVERWHELMED GOD—THE STUDY OF THE BRIDEGROOM'S EMOTIONS

You have ravished my heart, my sister, my spouse... (Song of Solomon 4:9 NKJV).

One of the most important studies we could explore is on the emotions of God. We will need to do this as we pursue gazing upon His beauty.

How does God feel when He sees and thinks of us? The right understanding of that question will change our emotional makeup forever. Our basic need as human beings is the need to feel loved and accepted. If this need is not met, we experience rejection. Many times we feel rejected by people. But usually that is caused by a wrong perception of how a person feels and thinks of us.

How then can we get out of this situation of feeling unloved and rejected? One way to resolve this is to study the emotions and feelings of the person whom we perceive to be prejudiced toward us. To our surprise, many times we find out that contrary to what we thought, the person—who we thought disliked us—has in fact affection for us.

Let's say you are in a job situation and have become very insecure with your boss. You misinterpret some of his actions, and your conclusion is that he does not like you. As a result you feel rejected and insecure. Then your boss realizes how you feel, and the truth is that he likes you very much. Now suppose that he has the ability to open his heart and then show you his favorable emotions and feelings toward you. By his actions and words he is saying, "See, these are my good feelings toward you; study them." As you study them, what would happen to you? Your emotional makeup would change. From feeling rejected and insecure, you would begin to feel loved and accepted. You would feel the change in your emotion as you discovered the real feelings of the person whom you thought did not like you.

GOD UNVEILS HIS HEART

No one can literally open their hearts to show what's on the inside, but in a way, I believe that is what God does for us in Song of Solomon where it says, "You have ravished my heart, my sister, my spouse…" (Song of Sol. 4:9 NKJV). This is God unveiling His heart for us and saying, "Look! This is My ravished heart. Study it because this is what I feel for you when I see you and think of you."

One of the definitions of *ravished* is "to be overwhelmed with deep, pleasurable feelings or emotions." God wants us to study His heart and to discover that in His heart He is overwhelmed with deep, pleasurable feelings and emotions for us.

When the reality of that truth starts to sink in—the reality that the God of the universe is overcome with deep delight over us—our emotional makeup changes dramatically. We start to feel loved and accepted by the Lord, who has strong emotions and feelings. As we have studied His pleasurable feelings toward us let's then start to imagine all His good and precious thoughts toward us.

How precious to me are Your thoughts, O God! How vast is the sum of them! Were I to count them, they would outnumber the grains of sand...(Psalm 139:17-18).

According to this verse, all God's precious thoughts outnumber the grains of sand. That means His precious thoughts for you would at least outnumber the grains of sand on one of the beaches in the world. So the next time you are at the beach pick up a grain, hold it between your fingers, and look at it. Remind yourself that this grain of sand represents one of God's good and precious thoughts toward you. Then sit down, find a glass, and drop the grain of sand into it. Take another grain and tell yourself, *this grain represents one of God's precious thoughts for me, when I was formed in my mother's womb.* Then take another grain and say, *this represents one of God's precious thoughts as I was born into this world.* Then keep doing it until you fill up the entire glass.

It has been estimated that one handful of sand contains approximately 10,000 grains of sand. So as you take a handful of sand and drop it grain by grain into the glass, consider that each grain represents one of God's precious thoughts toward you. And consider that one handful of sand represents 10,000 of God's precious thoughts for you. As the glass becomes full stand up, gaze across the beach, and realize that you have just started to own some of the depth of the love of God, contained in His precious thoughts.

We have a God of strong feelings and emotions. Those strong feelings and emotions toward us compelled Him to sacrifice His only Son. Have you ever thought about the pain that God felt seeing His Son being slowly tortured and eventually dying? What force is so strong that a father or mother would allow their only child to be tortured and killed in front of them? That force we do not possess. How could we in any situation be willing to sacrifice our children? But God was able to do it because there was a force so strong that allowed Him to go through the pain of giving up His only Son. That force was His love for you and me, as we read in the Book of John, "For God so loved the world that He gave His one and only Son" (John 3:16). This is not a weak love; this is strong, passionate, and forceful.

As we are drawn into this love and captured by His beauty, we start to seek His face. That this happens is almost too incredible to be true. Love begins to awaken, and being captivated by His beauty we seek His face. Our gaze into His eyes in response to His love, leads Him to express to us, "Turn your eyes from me; they overwhelm me" (Song of Sol. 6:5).

How is this possible? The God who created the universe with just His words, the God who has seen kingdoms rise and fall, who is not in the slightest way overwhelmed by all the great armies or wars or rulers through history, how could He be overwhelmed by us? I think what takes place is that God is overwhelmed by Himself, by His own strong feelings and emotions, but they are triggered by us.

We have a lovesick God. I don't know if you have been in love. But if you have, you know there *are* strong emotions going on inside. And if the object of your love turns, looks, and smiles—or even better, touches you—what happens then? You are overwhelmed on the inside. This gives us a hint of how God must feel.

This is an incredible thought: as we mature in love, and come to the place where we do not only receive love but also return our love to God, there is such power that triggers His heart that our love overwhelms Him.

Have you thought of God as lovesick? When we reach out to Him and say, "I love you," He is overwhelmed with strong feelings and emotions. This may be what John experienced when he was taken to the throne room of God. He said that out from the throne came "flashes of lightning, rumblings and peals of thunder" (Rev. 4:5). Could it be that John was experiencing some of the strong emotions of an overwhelmed God, coming out toward him as he entered that place? Could it be that God was so excited that one of His children had responded to the invitation to "come up here" that He was overwhelmed with strong feelings, and they went out toward John in the form of rumblings and thunder?

Our Love Is His Inheritance

We respond to his invitation to draw near to Him. This act of love is then His inheritance in us. We like to talk about our inheritance in Him, but do you know He has an inheritance that He is seeking too?

> *I pray also that the eyes of your heart may be enlightened in order that you may know the hope to which He has called you, the riches of His glorious inheritance in the saints* (Ephesians 1:18).

I used to read that and really interpret it as our inheritance in Him. But that is not what it is saying; it speaks about His glorious inheritance in us. What can we give Him that He is longing for from us, which He considers His inheritance in the saints? I believe that inheritance is our voluntary love.

This is His great inheritance. To have a people called the Bride, giving Him her free and voluntary love. When this happens, He is overwhelmed because that was the purpose of the whole creation–to bring forth a creation outside of the Godhead that would give love freely back to Him.

One of the important questions that pastors should ask themselves is this: does Jesus have an inheritance in the church under my care? As pastors, our goal is not to nourish nice, respectable believers–reading their Bibles, saying their prayers, and giving tithes. Our goal is to make sure that our people will not only understand their inheritance in God, but He will also have His inheritance in them. Then we will become a Church awakened in love, not only asking for yet another blessing, but pursuing God because we desire Him. We should be awakened to desire, following that longing, which leads us to His face. Our love is His inheritance in the saints.

This is the journey of desire. A strange verse in Song of Solomon says, "…do not arouse or awaken love until it so desires" (Song of Sol. 2:7). I have struggled to understand what this means, and I thought it meant we were to try to awaken love for God. What I have come to understand is this: we can't get people to pursue God before desire is awakened. If we try without desire it is dead religion. First and foremost, desire has to be awakened before anyone can set out on his or her journey of love. And desire is awakened by the study of the emotions and thoughts of God.

EXPERIENCING THE EMOTIONS OF GOD

Our pursuit does not stop with the study of God's emotions. The glory of the Gospel is not only that we can study them, but that we can actually experience the emotions of God. In other words, we can feel on the inside what God feels for us. In Colossians, Paul tells us:

> *The mystery that has been kept hidden for ages and generations, but is now disclosed to the saints. To them God has chosen to make known among the Gentiles the glorious riches of this mystery, which is Christ in you, the hope of glory* (Colossians 1:26-27).

This mystery is the reality of Christ in us, which is our hope for the coming glory. However, it is also our glory today. The fact that Christ is in us makes possible the reality of an experience on the inside.

In the Oscar-winning movie, *Chariots of Fire*, we follow Eric Liddell in his quest for an Olympic gold medal during the 1924 Summer Olympics in Paris. Later in life he became a missionary to China. One of the well-known lines is his response to his sister, when she asked if he was not spending too much time on his running, compared to missions work. "God made me fast, and when I run I feel His pleasure," is Liddell's famous reply. My question then is, "How did Eric Liddell feel God's pleasure?" Was it a physical experience when he was running along the beach, with the wind blowing against his face? Or was it an actual feeling inside him?

As we saw in Song of Solomon 4:9, God has pleasurable feelings toward us, and Eric Liddell claimed he felt this pleasure, which is also expressed in Romans, "...God has poured out His love in our hearts by the Holy Spirit" (Rom. 5:5). This is an incredible Word, regarding the burning love and passion of God that have now been poured out into our hearts. The pleasurable feelings He has when thinking about us, are not only there for us to study. They have now been poured out into our hearts, so that we can feel inside of us what God feels for us.

What is the Word of God other than His burning feelings for you and me, expressed in words? These burning realities are not meant only to be studied in the pages of a book, but to be experienced in our hearts.

We are now moving into a dimension that we as human beings in our interpersonal relationships can never enter into. Imagine that you hold strong feelings in your heart for a person. Then you share them with the person involved, and even write them down. But the recipient of your feelings has a hard time believing you. Faced with that situation you may feel helpless—wishing that if only you could put your hand inside your heart, bring out your strong feelings for that person, and literally put them inside that person's heart, then that person would feel inside your strong emotions for them. So then, that person would believe your real feelings. But of course, all you can do is merely express your feelings by speaking or writing them down.

Jesus on the other hand, is inviting us to cross that barrier into something much deeper. From before the dawn of time, the persons of the Trinity have existed in unity and union, sharing their love for one another. They have experienced on the inside the deep, common feelings and emotions each of them has nursed for the other. We are being called to enter into this dimension of unity, "just as You are in Me and I am in You. May they also be in Us…"(John 17:21).

The union between man and woman is just a shadow of this unity. It is a faded picture pointing to a much greater reality. This reality is not an experience of a physical union; it is an actual union of hearts, where our feelings for each other are truly experienced on the inside.

"Christ in us" is a mystery that has been kept hidden from ages past, but it is now being revealed. This then also becomes the heart of what the bridal message is all about.

Questions for Reflection

1. Have you taken time to meditate on God's precious thoughts for you? Can you picture yourself filling up a glass with 10,000 grains of sand, with each grain representing one of God's precious thoughts for you?

2. List examples in your life, which reflect God's love for you. What do you think are the benefits of cultivating a grateful attitude in our lives?

3. How does expressing our love verbally uplift our souls? How can we practice the expression of the psalmist when he said, "Praise the Lord, O my soul, and forget not all His benefits" (Ps. 103:2)?

Chapter 4

THE FLAME OF LOVE—THE PASSION OF THE BRIDAL GENERATION

Place me like a seal over your heart, like a seal on your arm; for love is as strong as death, its jealousy unyielding as the grave. It burns like blazing fire, like a mighty flame (Song of Solomon 8:6).

Almost ten years ago, I received this verse including verse 7, but only recently have I grasped its meaning. My late wife and I had these two verses engraved on our wedding rings. We felt God gave these verses to us, though we still did not understand them then. It really helped our understanding to know that commentaries considered these verses as the climax of Song of Solomon and that it described marital love at its strongest.

Then I heard that as Mike Bickle was meditating on Song of Solomon 8:6 in his office, for the first time the presence of the Lord suddenly came in a special way. While experiencing this, the phone rang and Bob Jones was on the line (a prophetic man in his church). Jones said that he had just heard the audible voice of the Lord and that the Lord was about to give Mike Bickle his life's mandate, found in Song of Solomon 8:6. Jones said that God was going to call

His people to it. And He was going to do this in the Body of Christ worldwide.[1] So what is special about this verse? What is it all about?

THE GREAT COMMISSION AND
THE GREAT COMMANDMENT

God has given us the great commission and the great commandment. The great commission is found in Matthew chapter 28, "Go make disciples of all nations" (see Matt. 28:18-20). That is our mandate, but who of us can do that? On our own none of us can. We can't fulfill the great commission unless the Lord enables us to do it. That is why He commanded His disciples to wait in Jerusalem until they received the Holy Spirit who would enable them to fulfill the great commission (see Acts 1:4-8). Jesus did not give them a commission and then leave without giving them the ability to fulfill it.

Understanding this principle, let's look at the great commandment. "Love the Lord with all your heart and with all your soul and with all your mind and with all your strength" (Mark 12:30). The second part of this commandment is to "love your neighbor as yourself. There is no commandment greater than these" (Mark 12:31).

But who of us can fulfill this? None of us, at least we cannot in our own strength. As He gave the power of the Holy Spirit to enable us to fulfill the great commission, what did He give to enable us to fulfill the great commandment? I believe He gave us the fire of love—the flame of the Holy Spirit—to enable us to fulfill it. God is love, but at the same time He is fire! "For our 'God is a consuming fire'" (Heb. 12:29).

So how do we reconcile these two—love and fire? God is love, but that love is so strong and passionate that when He is going to express the deep love and yearnings of His heart, the only way that it can be fully brought forth is as a burning flame. God's love is so intense, so passionate that it has become fire.

That is how He loves us, and He then commands us to love Him in return, calling us to love Him with the same intense love. He is looking for that fiery love that He has for us, to see if it is also burning in our hearts for Him.

I have made You known to them, and will continue to make You known in order that the love You have for Me may be in them and that I Myself may be in them (John 17:26).

This is Jesus finishing His high priestly prayer, and He ends it with an incredible request to the Father that the same fiery love, which the Father has for Him, may be in the disciples. He also explains how it will start to burn there. It is by Him making the Father known to them. When the Holy Spirit starts to reveal the beauty of God to our hearts, our hearts will be captured by Him and start burning.

We also receive this flame of fire through prayer, and that is what Song of Solomon 8:6 is all about. It is a prayer that the flame of love may be like a seal on the heart of the believer, a fire that enables us to be fiery lovers of God. Then when this fire of love burns in our hearts, Song of Solomon tells us:

Many waters cannot quench love; rivers cannot wash it away. If one were to give all the wealth of his house for love, it would be utterly scorned (Song of Solomon 8:7).

Water naturally quenches fire. But the fire mentioned here is a supernatural fire. When it burns in the heart, the waters of pain and difficulty and the rivers of persecution cannot wash it away. As we pray for this flame of fire to burn in our hearts, the Holy Spirit will come upon us and seal our hearts with the fire of love. "Having believed, you were marked in Him with a seal, the promised Holy Spirit" (Eph. 1:13). This seal is the same seal that Song of Solomon 8:6 speaks about; it is what the disciples received on the day of Pentecost.

THE WIND, FIRE, AND WINE

As I have come to understand, the disciples received the Holy Spirit in three different forms at the day of Pentecost: as wind, fire, and wine. *Wind* represents the power of God to enable them to be witnesses. *Wine* represents the joy of the Lord to gladden their hearts.

And finally, *fire* was the flame of love that would enable them to be fiery lovers of God.

We may have misinterpreted the tongues of fire that were descending on them. We may have thought these tongues of fire were a sign that they would become fiery preachers. But "tongues of fire" is an expression used to describe what fire looks like. And I believe it was not their tongues that would be set on fire but their hearts.

If we look to the Bible for clarification, we find that the only other place it speaks about "tongues of fire" is in connection with consuming straw, meaning that it is a way to describe what fire looks like when it burns. In Isaiah we read:

> *Therefore, as **tongues of fire** lick up straw and as dry grass sinks down in the flames, so their roots will decay and their flowers blow away like dust* (Isaiah 5:24).

So at the day of Pentecost, or P-Day, the disciples received three P's:

- Power—the wind to enable them to fulfill the great commission.

- Passion—the fire of love to enable them to fulfill the great commandment.

- Pleasure—the wine to gladden their hearts and enable them to enjoy God.

THE WORD IS FIRE

Finally, we may also receive this fire of love through meditation on the Word of God. The disciples on the road to Emmaus asked each other, "Were not our hearts burning within us while He talked with us on the road and opened the Scriptures to us?" (See Luke 24:32.) This was Jesus revealing the Word to them, and as a result their hearts were burning.

Scripture has the ability to set our hearts on fire because it is fire itself. As the prophet Jeremiah said:

But if I say, "I will not mention Him or speak any more in His name," His word is in my heart like a fire, a fire shut up in my bones. I am weary of holding it in; indeed, I cannot (Jeremiah 20:9).

In the Book of John we read, "In the beginning was the Word and the Word was with God, and the Word was God" (John 1:1). The Word was God—and God is fire, which means that the Word is fire. "In Him was life, and that life was the light of men" (John 1:4). We have mostly perceived the fire of God as the fire of judgment, and that is one side of it. Fire can destroy, but the other side of fire is to bring life and light.

What is the source of light? Fire. As we know, the sun is a ball of fire so we can rightly say that fire then becomes the source of life. So it is both the source of life and destruction. With this understanding, the words in John 1:4 take on a deeper meaning because we can also say that in Him was fire and that fire was the light of men.

How do we receive this fire in our hearts? We now understand that the Word is fire. It dwelled in eternity past. Then it was cloaked with words and syllables and was put in the pages of a book. But it is not meant to stay there. These eternal, burning truths and realities about God are longing to break forth from these pages to become flames of fire again. These eternal, burning realities that dwelled outside time and space—which for a moment needed to be wrapped in words and syllables, so they could enter this world—long to be unwrapped again, to become fire in our hearts.

Dana Candler expresses this well in her excellent book *Deep Unto Deep*. Writing about eternal spiritual realities she says:

> They begin as words and end as burning realities. They start as concepts but become experiences in God. They expand within us and stretch their boundaries far beyond the natural confinement of time and space. They are without limit, for they are living truths of love that eternally remains. They begin as words, for syllables and concepts are the package surrounding very real realities. Yet when these fiery realities wrapped in words are accepted

into the chamber of our beings, they find their rightful vessel, and in time, the titles that once held them are cast aside and no longer needed. The living substance now abides within the human heart. The reality of "God is love" is eternal, yet the words and syllables come only as temporary service to tote the reality around until it finds its home within the secret place of the human heart.

I imagine the Holy Spirit, the wind of God, catches these words and concepts with His wings, rushing them into the center of my being. There He breathes upon them, and as I ponder upon them, mulling over them with love and meditation, they eventually ignite into a living flame. At this point, there is no longer need for words or concepts. They have done their duty. Language is left behind smiling, for she has accomplished her God-ordained responsibility, and now the flame burns on its own. She remains within the boundaries of what can be communicated, while the burning reality that once required ideas and concepts to be understood now takes me upon its wings into the realm of love far surpassing knowledge and ascends eternally into the great Beyond.[2]

Our aim, through prayer and meditation, is that this Word becomes fire in our hearts. Let me give you an example of how that may happen. The sun burns and gives light, but if you concentrate that light under a magnifying glass it transforms into fire. In the same way, the Word that once burned as the sun, was given into this world through the Bible, and it became the light of the world. Remember, as we concentrate light through a magnifying glass it transforms into fire. In the same way, this happens when we meditate on the Word, which is the way God has given us to concentrate the light of the Word. As we meditate on the Word directing it toward our hearts, it will ignite and burn in our hearts.

THE BURNING ONES

To be burning ones is our call and our destiny. We talk much about being the light of the world and even have songs about it, but we also need to talk about why we shine—and that is because we burn.

When Jesus spoke again to the people, He said, "I am the light of the world. Whoever follows Me will never walk in darkness, but will have the light of life" (John 8:12).

In Matthew chapter 5, Jesus says, "You are the light of the world" (Matt. 5:14). When Jesus described John the Baptist, He said that John was the greatest man born of a woman (see Matt. 11:11). And then we hear Jesus talk of John this way, "John was a lamp that burned and gave light, and you chose for a time to enjoy his light" (John 5:35).

John gave light because he burned. Our focus is usually that he was a shining lamp. But the reason John was shining was because he burned. He was one of the burning ones.

John was a forerunner for Jesus' first coming, to prepare people for the coming of the Lord. But just as he was raised up as one who burned to prepare people for the first coming of Christ, God is also raising up an army of forerunners today, to prepare people for the Second Coming. He is raising up many burning ones at the end of the age. And one of their main characteristics will be that they are burning.

Regarding the apostles of old, have you noticed that they were always depicted in paintings with halos over their heads? They were shining, and they shined because they burned. We also read that Peter's shadow healed the sick. But if we look at the original Greek it says it was an outshining that came from Peter, which healed the sick. This expression has been translated as "shadow" but it is more correct to say that the "light shining out from him" healed the sick.

To illustrate this point let me tell you of a friend's experience during a YWAM gathering some years ago. One of those present was asked to pray, and as he prayed my friend saw that his whole face started to shine and fire went out of his eyes. She also saw a wind around his mouth. A person who happened to pass by the room as this took place, related afterward that as he heard this person pray, the Holy Spirit came over him. He experienced healing from a sickness from which he was suffering! He did not see anything; he just experienced it. However, my friend had her eyes opened for a little while to the activity of the Holy Spirit, and she saw the fire and the wind going out to heal this person.

The interesting thing was that the fire did not come from the mouth but from the eyes, and it was the wind—which is the power of the Spirit—that she saw around the mouth. I believe it was the same light that went out from Peter that healed the sick. The eyes of some people around him were opened to see what happened in the spiritual realm. So they saw that the disciples were surrounded with light. That's the reason why they were painted that way—with light shining around them, especially coming from their faces.

This was also what Peter, James, and John experienced when they were taken up to the Mount of Transfiguration. Their eyes were opened to see Jesus as He really is:

> *There He was transfigured before them. His face shone like the sun, and His clothes became as white as the light* (Matthew 17:2).

Our calling to burn and shine is not just symbolic. Literally, flames of fire came on the disciples. It was not a natural flame or a natural light, but nevertheless it was still real. It is a spiritual reality, an actual flame and an actual light, and on occasion our eyes will be opened to actually see it, as my friend experienced. Jesus is longing to come to His Church and find this fire burning. In Revelation, it says:

> *I turned around to see the voice that was speaking to me. And when I turned I saw seven golden lampstands, and among the lampstands was someone "like a son of man" dressed in a robe reaching down to His feet and with a golden sash around His chest* (Revelation 1:12-13).

Here we find Jesus where He loves to be, among His lampstands. And, according to Scripture, the lampstands are the seven churches (see

Rev. 1:20). Why are the churches symbolized as lampstands? Probably because they were to be lampstands so that the flame of the Holy Spirit could burn in them. We see in Revelation chapter 2 that Jesus is rebuking the church at Ephesus (see Rev. 2:1-5). She was rebuked for forsaking her first love, and what was her first love other than the fire of love burning in her lampstand? This is made clear where it says that if she does not repent He will come and remove her lampstand (see Rev. 2:5). Why would He do that? Because if the fire of love is not burning anymore, there is no need for the lampstand.

THE END OF THE AGE

I believe that as we approach the end of the age, the issue of believers being burning and shining lamps will become a central theme. This will begin to manifest, as the Church understands the bridal message. This was explicitly expressed in the parable of the ten virgins Jesus talked about. "At that time the kingdom of heaven will be like ten virgins who took their lamps and went out to meet their bridegroom" (Matt. 25:1). The wise virgins are those who are burning and shining prepared to meet their bridegroom. They have to put oil in their lamp, which is a symbol of the Holy Spirit so that the flame of love could burn in their lamps.

At the end of the age, I believe the focus will be on the bridal message and on having the fire of love burning in our lamps. This parable is about ten virgins: five of them were wise, and five were foolish. But the issue is really about burning and shining. Why were they to have *oil* in their lamps, which is a symbol of the Holy Spirit? The point is that they were to have oil so that the flame of love could burn in their lamps.

We can see this is the issue in Daniel 12 where the focus is the end of the age. We read about what will characterize believers at that time, "Those who are wise will shine like the brightness of the heavens…" (Dan. 12:3). Why will they shine? Because they have been wise and bought oil for their lamps, so that the fire of love can burn in their hearts.

Becoming the Bride of Christ in the Last Days

In the Book of Isaiah, we find a great promise, which many believe speaks prophetically about the end of the age:

Arise, shine, for your light has come, and the glory of the Lord rises upon you. See, darkness covers the earth and thick darkness is over the peoples, but the Lord rises upon you and His glory appears over you. Nations will come to your light, and kings to the brightness of your dawn (Isaiah 60:1-3).

This tells us that at the end of the age when darkness covers the world, the Church will arise and shine because she is burning. In his book, *The Days of His Presence,* Francis Frangipane shares a prophetic experience that confirms this understanding:

> Much of what I believe concerning the end of the age comes from a vision the Lord gave me in 1971. In it, I saw a city blanketed by a deep, thick darkness. A feeling of great hopelessness and desolation prevailed over the region. Like the darkness that descended as a judgment over Egypt, this also was a darkness that could be felt (Exodus 10:21).
>
> Those whom I was with were outside the city. We had been "baptized" in a glorious and powerful light. In the vision, I actually experienced the power of this light surging up from my innermost being and out through my hands. A visible splendor shone from our bodies, especially our faces.
>
> Suddenly, people by tens of thousands started streaming out of the darkness. As they approached, they were calling on the name of the Lord. We prayed and laid our hands on them and they, too, received the light.
>
> I lay awake until dawn pondering the vision. It had been my habit to read the Word of God immediately upon waking. As the morning light began to enter my bedroom, I opened my Bible to begin my next

reading. There, for the first time in my young spiritual life, I read Isaiah 60....

It said that darkness would cover the earth, but the glory of the Lord will rise upon His people! The words bolted into my eyes like lightning, then shook my insides like thunder. It was as though I had actually stepped into a Bible verse and seen its fulfillment. The Holy Spirit and the Word working together revealed that, at the end of the age, the glory of the Lord would be manifested in His people—and multitudes would come to the Lord as a result![3]

OUR ETERNAL DESTINY

It is our eternal destiny to live with the Godhead, who shines and burns. Isaiah saw this and wrote, "Who of us can dwell with everlasting burning?" (Isa. 33:14). Who can dwell with everlasting burning, meaning the Trinity. Those who, from ages past, have dwelled together in burning passion for each other—with fiery love for each other but also for us—are longing for us to join them. But how can we live there? Only when we have become flames ourselves. Only when we become burning ones ourselves, can we dwell with everlasting burning. Only flames of fire will survive fire, for everything will burn up except the living flames.

There are many places where we can read of God and His light. For example, Revelation chapter 22 says, "There will be no more night. They will not need the light of a lamp or the light of the sun, for the Lord God will give them light" (Rev. 22:5). And chapter 21 of Revelation says, "The city does not need the sun or the moon to shine on it, for the glory of God gives it light, and the Lamb is its lamp" (Rev. 21:23).

Now look at Jesus' last description of Himself:

I, Jesus, have sent My angel to give you this testimony for the churches. I am the Root and the Offspring of David, and the bright Morning Star (Revelation 22:16).

Jesus describes Himself as "the bright Morning Star." But what does Scripture say of us? "Then the righteous will shine like the sun in the kingdom of their Father. He who has ears, let him hear" (Matt. 13:43). The Bible says that we will also shine like the sun. How does the sun shine? It shines because it burns. Brothers and sisters, this is our destiny: to burn in the Kingdom of our Father forever and ever.

Even today, the everlasting burning is calling us to burn with the flames of holy passion and love. We are being called to become burning ones. To become those who burn with the holy flames of love, so that we can be a light and give life in this sick and dying world.

With this new understanding, our prayers become Song of Solomon 8:6. We pray that He will seal us with the seal of fire upon our hearts, so that we may become wholehearted lovers of God and love Him with the same fiery love with which He loves us.

Endnotes

1. Mike Bickle, CD teaching series, "Encountering Jesus–A Prophetic History and Perspectives About the Endtimes," (FOTB 2003), CD 6.

2. Dana Candler, *Deep Unto Deep: The Journey of His Embrace* (Kansas, MO: Forerunner Publishing, 2004), 138-139.

3. Francis Frangipane, *The Days of His Presence* (Cedar Rapids, IA: Arrow Publications, 1995), 24-25.

Questions for Reflection

1. How did this chapter describe the way to get a burning heart? How will you develop yours?

2. How can we overcome the circumstances of life, which try to quench our love for God?

Chapter 5

Pleasure Forevermore—The Bridegroom Fast

How can the guests of the bridegroom mourn while He is with them?
The time will come when the bridegroom will be taken from them;
then they will fast (Matthew 9:15).

Contrary to what many think, the New Testament paradigm of fasting and the whole focus of a fasted lifestyle is not about self-denial, but of experiencing the "superior pleasures of the Gospel," as Mike Bickle puts it.

As the shorter catechism says, "The chief end of man is to glorify God and to enjoy Him forever." Noted author and Bible teacher John Piper has rewritten this to say, "The chief end of man is to glorify God by enjoying Him forever."[1] It is by enjoying Him that we give Him glory. How can a child bring glory to his father if the only reason the child comes to him is out of obligation, and not because he enjoys being with him?

Our chief end is to enjoy God. When we enjoy Him, we burst into praise, much like we burst into praise if we hear a song that we like or see a painting that strikes our heart. Consider a chef: the degree to which we honor and bring joy to him, is proportional to the degree to which we truly enjoy his food. The more we enjoy and find pleasure in his creations, the more he is honored and praised.

Jonathan Edwards wrote, "God is glorified not only by His glory being seen, but by its being rejoiced in." And Sam Storms says:

> The treasure which is God, is glorified not only by His glory being seen, but by its being rejoiced in.... The treasure which is God, is most glorified in and by you when your pleasure in Him is maximal and optimal.[2]

We all seek pleasure. Contrary to our traditional understanding, this desire is given to us by God. Our goal is not to smother it, but rather to do whatever we can to satisfy it. Dr. Larry Crabb contributed the foreword to Storm's book, *Pleasure Evermore*. In it, Crabb writes:

> Too many Christians struggle against *sinful* passions (which we should do) by running away from *all* passions (which we should not do). We are like children who grudgingly eat our spinach of obedience, hoping someday we will receive a cookie.

> But the battle to *resist* pleasure and instead do what is right is not the core battle Christianity introduces into our lives. The core battle is to believe that the Eternal Community of God is a party that we all long to attend and to discover and freely indulge our deepest passions for their kind of fun.[3]

Superior pleasure is found only in God's presence, and that pleasure is eternal (see Ps. 16:11). That is the pleasure we want to take hold of, so that we can be fully satisfied. We will not be satisfied with the passing pleasures of sin, or even with good God-given legitimate pleasures, which certainly have their place—like the enjoyment of a well-prepared meal, good quality movies, or any other recreation that you enjoy. No matter how good and enjoyable any of that may be, it is still a fleeting experience.

Our main desire and goal should be not for what is temporary, but for what is eternal. "So we fix our eyes not on what is seen, but on what is unseen. For what is seen is temporary, but what is unseen is eternal" (2 Cor. 4:18).

This is what will fully satisfy our longing for pleasure. When it says at His "right hand are pleasures forevermore," I believe it can imply two things (see Ps. 16:11 NKJV). First, as we enter that position of being close to Him, we enjoy the atmosphere emanating from His very being. Second, we find pleasure forevermore in Jesus who sits at His right hand.

How do we enter this realm of experiencing the superior pleasure? Our basic problem in searching for superior pleasure is that we are too easily satisfied. In the words of C.S. Lewis:

> We are half-hearted creatures, fooling about with drink and sex and ambition when infinite joy is offered us, like an ignorant child who wants to go on making mud pies in a slum because he cannot imagine what is meant by the offer of a holiday at the sea. We are far too easily pleased.[4]

We are pleased and satisfied either by the deceiving pleasure of fleeting sin or even with good, God-given, legitimate pleasures. Therefore, to be able to enjoy superior pleasure, we have to abandon these inferior pleasures. Why should we abandon them? Because God created us for superior pleasure and not for temporary deceiving pleasure that leaves us all empty in the end. The call to repentance from sinful pleasure is not the call to repentance from *our longing* to seek pleasure. It is the call to repent from being satisfied too early and settling for too little.

Then we have good and legitimate pleasures, which belong to the temporary, visible realm. If we do not properly train our spiritual senses, they may be easily drowned by our preoccupation with good and legitimate pleasures of life. That is why the call to the fasted lifestyle is so important. It includes, among other things, fasting from food—but not only that. It is a call to deny good, legitimate pleasures for a season in the pursuit of superior pleasure.

All pleasure seekers need to deny themselves some pleasures in the pursuit of what they consider superior pleasure. The one who seeks the pleasure of a well-fit and trained body, has to say no to what would be considered the lesser pleasure of an enticing slice of cake. Or a man in love has to give up the lesser pleasure, of sitting home reading a good book or watching a movie, for the superior pleasure of spending time with his beloved.

The seeking of one thing will always be at the expense of many other things, but the focus should not be on what we need to deny ourselves. Rather, the focus should be on what we are seeking. "It is written: 'Man does not live on bread alone, but on every word that comes from the mouth of God'" (Matt. 4:4).

The Scripture says that we do not live on bread alone, but on every word that comes from the mouth of God. But many times our spiritual appetites are suppressed because we are too busy indulging our physical appetites. Sometimes we need to suppress our physical appetites to awaken, call forth, and indulge our spiritual appetites.

I love going to banquet tables—to taste and try all that is offered. And when I am at a banquet, I don't suddenly read the newspaper or work on my laptop, and then take a bite of all the delicious food in between working or reading. I can do that at home as I read my morning paper, drink my coffee, and eat some cereal—but not at a banquet.

Likewise, the Lord sometimes wants us to have and enjoy a spiritual banquet. He wants to prepare a banquet table for us. And when you are there enjoying it, you won't suddenly take out your newspaper or turn on the television.

During regular days we have our breakfast, read our Bible, pray, and maybe watch the morning news, and then we are off on our way to work. But the banquet times in the Spirit are different. You are there at the table for hours or days, just focusing on getting all you can, indulging your spiritual appetite. Your physical appetite has to be set aside for a time. Neil Armstrong said, "Eating is the granddaddy of all appetites." But when we speak of the physical appetite, we are not only talking about food but also about entertainment, the Internet, newspapers, fellowship with others, and for married couples it can include abstinence from sexual intimacy (see 1 Cor. 7:5).

By fasting, we also break the power of overindulgence. God has given us good and legitimate pleasures to enjoy. But these were not meant to be the end in themselves, but to show us the way toward ultimate pleasure.

If they become an end in themselves we can easily overindulge, which is the red light God has given us. When we are fasting, we break the spirit of overindulgence in our lives, and it brings us back to the pursuit of superior pleasure. This becomes the place where we can take a free fall into the river of His delight.

In Psalms, we read, "They feast on the abundance of Your house; You give them drink from Your river of delights" (Ps. 36:8). In this river we are called to fully indulge ourselves where overindulgence does not exist. It is the only place where we will be fully satisfied because this river is God Himself. Even God's good gifts leave us empty, if they become an end in themselves. Sam Storms puts it this way:

> When it comes to satisfying our spiritual appetites, *there is no such thing as excess.* There are no restraints placed on us by God. There are no rules of temperance or laws requiring moderation or boundaries beyond which we cannot go in seeking to enjoy him. We need never pause to inquire whether we've crossed a line or become overindulgent.[5]

The psalmist writes, "You prepare a table before me..." (Ps. 23:5). As we are sitting down at the table the Lord has prepared for us, partaking of all the spiritual blessings He serves, we are also entering a form of what we may call the bridegroom fast.

THE BRIDEGROOM FAST

How can the guests of the bridegroom mourn while He is with them? The time will come when the bridegroom will be taken from them; then they will fast (Matthew 9:15).

Jesus introduces the bridegroom fast in Matthew 9:14-17. It is interesting to note that this is the place where Jesus chooses to reveal His deepest identity when it comes to His relationship with us. He basically says, "I am the Bridegroom."

You may ask, "Is it not more important that He is my Savior and the Lord of the universe?" No, for He came to save us because He was a bridegroom coming for His Bride. If you were to marry the Prince of Norway, the most important thing for you would be that he was *your* bridegroom and not the fact that he was a prince.

Jesus reveals His deepest identity as our Bridegroom in the context of fasting. Why is that? It should tell us that fasting is important. After Jesus reveals His identity, He goes on to introduce the bridegroom fast—the New Testament paradigm of fasting.

John's disciples come to Him asking about fasting from the Old Testament paradigm. Jesus, seeing where they are coming from, answers their question using language they can understand. He says:

> *How can the guests of the bridegroom mourn while He is with them? The time will come when the bridegroom will be taken from them; then they will fast* (Matthew 9:15).

Here, Jesus is using the word *mourning* interchangeably with *fasting*. In the Old Testament paradigm, fasting and mourning were closely connected. In Joel 1:13-15, we see the connection between fasting, mourning, and sackcloth; it was in the context of preventing God's judgment. We also see some of this in Jonah chapter 3 and Esther 4:1-3.

I am not saying that this form of fasting does not have a place. But I believe Jesus introduces a new paradigm, when He says that the main reason for fasting after He leaves will be the bridegroom fast: *fasting not to prevent God's judgment but because we, as the Bride, are missing Jesus our Bridegroom.*

Jesus is saying that when He, the Bridegroom, is with His coming Bride, it is not a time of mourning but of joy. But when He leaves we will fast, and this fast will ultimately be broken when we meet again at the wedding table of the Lamb.

That is why the call to a fasted lifestyle is important. We are entering a fast together with Jesus, saying, "I am fasting until we meet again as an expression that I miss you. When we meet again we will break the fast together at the wedding table." It is not only we who are fasting; Jesus does it too. At the Passover meal just before Jesus left the disciples, He said this about the wine:

> *I tell you, I will not drink of this fruit of the vine from now on until that day when I drink it anew with you in my Father's kingdom* (Matthew 26:29).

Here we see that there is something in Heaven that Jesus will fast from until we meet Him at our wedding day. He basically says, "I will fast when I leave, and you, my Bride, will fast." When He left, He said that we would fast and then we would break the fast together when we finally meet Him at the ultimate banquet table. Therefore, as Jesus entered into a fast to express that He misses us too, He then invites us to do the same.

So in practical terms, how do we enter this fast—the fasting until the Lord returns? There are different ways we can do this. One is to abstain from something and decide not to eat it until that day. Or it can also be by entering a lifestyle where you are fasting on a weekly or monthly basis until He returns.

As we start this fasted lifestyle, we also understand that it is not just about entering a fast together with Jesus but also taking part here and now in the fulfillment of the prophecy that Jesus spoke about: "Then they will fast." Every time we miss His presence, the means Jesus gave us to express it is through fasting.

The bridal generation is chosen to partake in the bridegroom fast. And in these last days this bridal generation will arise and enter into the ultimate dimension of this fast—that is, to usher His physical coming. It will be the Church entering what I call the Revelation 22:17 reality, which is the Spirit and the Bride saying, "Come."

This is the ultimate expression of the bridegroom fast. He knows that at the end of the age, the Church will enter into a revelation and experience as a mature Bride with a bridal heart.

What is the essence of a bridal heart? It is like a woman anticipating her bridegroom on their wedding day. This becomes her consuming passion, as all other concerns of life become secondary.

She has truly become a person of one thing. And she expresses this one desire through the "come prayer." The way Jesus told His disciples to say, "Come," was through the bridegroom fast. This was also the prayer He taught them to pray. When they asked how they should pray, He taught them the "come prayer": "Your kingdom come..." (Matt. 6:10).

Throughout the ages, that's what the Church has been praying. But as we all know, a kingdom without a king is no kingdom at all. So at the end of the age, one generation will not only pray for the Kingdom to come but, more importantly, for the King to come back.

THE NEW WINESKINS

In the last part of His teaching on the bridegroom fast, Jesus connects it with the importance of pouring new wine into new wineskins. I believe this especially relates to the endtime, when the church will enter into the reality of Revelation 22:17.

As the Bride comes before Him and cries, "Come," at the end of the age—just before His Second Coming—there has to be built up a new structure or wineskin to facilitate that cry to come forth. At the end of the age that cry will crescendo to 24 hours a day, 7 days a week, 365 days a year! It is going to be a yearlong cry for Him to come.

It's not just about saying, "Come." The "come prayer" then also becomes a prayer for the end-time harvest because that is one of the things that must take place before His coming. So then the end-time harvest in a way becomes not a goal in itself but one of the elements that stands between the Bride and her Bridegroom on their wedding day. Because of this, she gives herself to pray for the harvest, and that becomes one of the ways she expresses her cry, "Come."

The house of prayer then becomes the place where the Church, in any geographical area, comes together as one Bride crying out. As

Jesus sees just one Church in any given geographical area, He also sees only one Bride with many different local expressions. It's like the nation of Israel, which was divided into different tribes, each with their own uniqueness. This was how they lived their daily lives, but when it came to worship they all gathered together in the temple worshipping the Lord as one nation.

Today, I believe the Lord is gathering His people not only as one nation, but even more as one Bride to say, "Come." The Lord is also making a new wineskin, the house of prayer where we can come together as one Bride saying, "Come," expressed through the bridegroom fast until He returns. This becomes her consuming passion above all other concerns of life.

In conclusion, let's look at the connection between the house of prayer and the bridal message. In Isaiah, God declares the bridal message over the nation of Israel, and the blessings He will give her as He brings her back to Him from her backslidden state. "For your Maker is your husband–the Lord Almighty is His name" (Isa. 54:5). Then in Isaiah 56:4-6, the Lord gives a message to eunuchs and foreigners (Gentiles):

> *To them I will give within My temple and its walls a memorial and a name better than sons and daughters; I will give them an everlasting name that will not be cut off* (Isaiah 56:5).

God promises a name better than sons and daughters, and what is better, closer, and more intimate than a son or a daughter, other than a wife or a bride? Then we see in verse 7, which is one of the main verses on the house of prayer, how these people will be brought to Him:

> *These I will bring to My holy mountain and give them joy in My house of prayer. Their burnt offerings and sacrifices will be accepted on My altar; for My house will be called a house of prayer for all nations* (Isaiah 56:7).

Why will there be joy? There will be joy because of the bridal revelation. In Isaiah 62:2-5, we see the bridal message and the new name that we will receive. It is a name that indicates intimacy and one that is better than the name given to sons and daughters. "…You will be called Hephzibah, and your land Beulah; for the Lord will take delight in you, and your land will be married" (Isa. 62:4). *Hephzibah* means, "My delight is in her." It is the name He gives us for being His beloved and His delight as a Bride. We know that a name given to a bride is better than a name given to sons and daughters in the sense that the name given to a spouse speaks more of the union and intimacy of a couple.

In verse 5, we see even more clearly that the context is the bridal paradigm. "As a young man marries a maiden, so will your sons marry you; as a bridegroom rejoices over his bride, so will your God rejoice over you" (Isa. 62:5). Furthermore, as the bride flows with intimacy, a house of prayer is set night and day.

> *I have posted watchmen on your walls, O Jerusalem; they will never be silent day or night. You who call on the Lord, give yourselves no rest, and give Him no rest till He establishes Jerusalem and makes her the praise of the earth* (Isaiah 62:6-7).

The bridal message is what will bring joy in the house of prayer, to sustain it and enable it to run night and day. It is where the Bride meets with her Bridegroom, and then there will be joy and rejoicing (see Isa. 62:5). In Isaiah chapter 56, the promise of a new name or a deeper revelation of our identity as the Bride is promised in the context of the house of prayer (see Isa. 56:5-7). Therefore, the house of prayer does not just become a place to get answers to prayers for our needs, but a place where intimacy with God is expressed. Prayer then, becomes a delight only in the context of a bridal paradigm. Prayer is no longer a duty to endure. It is not a means to an end but an end in itself, as any bride longs for and enjoys talking to her bridegroom. (It is interesting to note that Mike Bickle, who is the main instrument in bringing the bridal message to the body of Christ, is also the founder of the International House of Prayer.)

It is within new wineskins that we can live out the bridegroom fast and say, "Come," through our fasting. Moreover, as we do, He will come with His presence into our lives for us to enjoy the Bridegroom's embrace. And eventually it is in that context that we will say not only "Come to me," but even "Come for me."

GLOBAL BRIDEGROOM FAST

Some years ago, I could honestly say that I could not yet hear the bridal cry of Revelation 22:17. But today, I am starting to hear this cry. It may only be a whisper today, compared to what it will become one day, but I believe it has begun.

One of the expressions of that cry is the global bridegroom fast for which Mike Bickle (from the International House of Prayer in Kansas City) and Lou Engle (founder of The Call) have taken the initiative. They are calling the Body of Christ worldwide to come together, every first Monday, Tuesday, and Wednesday in each month from January to November and seven days in December. This is a total of 40 days in a year. It is interesting that if you are fasting for 40 days in one year, you are actually giving to the Lord, not only the first days of each month, but also a tenth or a tithe of the entire year to seek Him in prayer and fasting.

This is a call for a solemn assembly—coming to the Lord in prayer and fasting, and basically saying, "Come." They are committed to do this until the Lord returns. Mike Bickle believes that eventually, there will be at least 100 million believers worldwide coming together the first days of each month saying, "Come." As this accelerates we will truly be able to say that we are starting to enter the Revelation 22:17 reality.

As this cry escalates, in the Father's perfect time, the sky will break and the Bridegroom will come for His waiting Bride.

ENDNOTES

1. John Piper, *Desiring God—Meditations of a Christian Hedonist* (Portland, OR: Multnomah Press, 1986), 14.

2. Sam Storms, *One Thing—Developing a Passion for the Beauty of God* (Scotland, Great Britain: Christian Focus Publications Ltd., 2004), 36.

3. Sam Storms, *Pleasure Evermore* (Colorado Springs, CO: NavPress, 2000), 9.

4. C.S. Lewis, *The Weight of Glory and Other Addresses* (Grand Rapids, MI: Eerdsman, 1965), 2.

5. Sam Storms, *One Thing—Developing a Passion for the Beauty of God* (Scotland, Great Britain: Christian Focus Publications Ltd., 2004), 27.

Questions for Reflection

1. What was your view of fasting in the past? What experiences have you had with it?

2. How did the bridegroom fast as a New Testament understanding enlighten you?

3. What steps will you take to build the reality of fasting into your life, and by doing so become part of the bridal generation that says, "Come"?

Chapter 6

THE BRIDE—THE IDENTITY OF THE BRIDAL GENERATION

Come, I will show you the bride, the wife of the Lamb (Revelation 21:9).

This is a prophetic word for our time. The Bride is about to be revealed for the whole earth to see. In First Corinthians we read that a "woman is the glory of man" (1 Cor. 11:7). We, as the Church, are that woman who is the glory of man–Christ Jesus, and He is about to show forth that glory for all to see. However before it occurs, the Church must first come to the understanding of her identity as the Bride. As she reaches that point, she will realize that she is at the heart of the very reason of the created order.

In his book, *Destined for the Throne*, Paul Billheimer writes:

> The universe, including this planet, was created for one purpose: to provide a suitable habitation for the human race. The human race was created in the image and likeness of God for the one purpose: to provide an eternal companion for the Son. After the

fall and promise of redemption through the coming Messiah, the Messianic Race was born and nurtured in order to bring the Messiah. And the Messiah came for one intent and only one: to give birth to His Church, thus to obtain His Bride. The Church, then—the called-out body of redeemed mankind—turns out to be the central object, the goal, not only of mundane history but of all that God has been doing in all realms, from all eternity.

...as the Lord of history, God is controlling all of its events, not only on earth but in all realms, to serve His purpose of bringing to maturity and eventually to enthronement with His Son, not angels or archangels, but the Church, His chosen Bride.[1]

These words from Billheimer are very strong, but are they true? Can we, mere human beings, look into the heart of God from before time began, to find out about the very reason for our existence? I believe we can!

Even if what we see are only glimpses, I believe that these glimpses are enough to give us an image of the Bride as the main reason of the created order. I say so because from the beginning of human existence He instituted marriage, which expresses the deepest form of relationship on earth. No other relationship can sufficiently mirror how intimately He wants that relationship with us to be other than marriage.

Let's revisit what was in the heart of God from eternity past. First Corinthians chapter 2 says:

We do, however, speak a message of wisdom among the mature, but not the wisdom of this age or of the rulers of this age, who are coming to nothing. No, we speak of God's secret wisdom, a wisdom that has been hidden and that God destined for our glory before time began. None of the rulers of this age understood it, for if they had, they would not have crucified the Lord of glory. However, as it is written: "No eye has seen, no ear has heard, no mind has conceived what God has prepared for those who love Him"—but God has revealed it to us by

His Spirit. The Spirit searches all things, even the deep things of God. For who among men knows the thoughts of a man except the man's spirit within him? In the same way no one knows the thoughts of God except the Spirit of God. We have not received the spirit of the world but the Spirit who is from God, that we may understand what God has freely given us (1 Corinthians 2:6-12).

And in the Book of Romans it says:

Now to Him who is able to establish you by my gospel and the proclamation of Jesus Christ, according to the revelation of the mystery hidden for long ages past (Romans 16:25).

In these two passages Paul is talking about a secret wisdom, from before time began; in Romans 16:25 he calls it a mystery. And this secret wisdom is so great that "no eye has seen, no ear has heard, no mind has conceived what God has prepared for those who love Him" (1 Cor. 2:9).

But now, this secret wisdom and these mysteries, which touched even the deep things of the heart of God, have started to be revealed to us through the Spirit "that we may understand what God has freely given us" (1 Cor. 2:12). If that is true, then the question arises: what are some of these mysteries and secrets that have been hidden in the heart of God?

THE GREAT MYSTERY OF THE AGES

If we look at Ephesians chapter 3, we see that Paul talks about this "mystery" four times in this chapter. And basically Paul says that the mystery is that through the Gospel, the Gentiles are now included together with Israel, in the promises of Christ (see Eph. 3:6).

Paul then goes on to talk about marriage in Ephesians 5:22-33. He says:

"For this reason a man will leave his father and mother and be united to his wife, and the two will become one flesh." This is a profound mystery—but I am talking about Christ and the church (Ephesians 5:31-32).

The *King James Version* of the Bible uses the word *great* instead of *profound*. Paul has been talking about the mystery in chapter 3, but in chapter 5 he starts to talk about the great mystery. And what is this great mystery that was not only a mystery, but a great and profound one? It is about marriage.

In Ephesians 5:31, Paul is quoting Genesis 2:24. And in verse 32, he is saying that what you have thought was about marriage between a man and a woman is really a prophetic declaration about how Christ would leave His father to be united to His Bride, the Church—to become one with her. This is the great mystery that was hidden from ages past, but it has now been revealed to his servants, the prophets.

Even before the Fall, marriage was a prophetic picture pointing toward Christ and His Bride. The Bride was already prophesied; this is clear Pauline teaching. The picture of marriage in Genesis 2:24 occurs before the prophetic picture of Jesus in Genesis 3:15, which is usually the one we understand as the first prophetic word about Jesus.

> *And I will put enmity between you and the woman, and between your offspring and hers; he will crush your head, and you will strike his heel* (Genesis 3:15).

This prophetic word speaks of how Jesus will crush the head of the snake. But this came after the Fall. However, from the apostle Paul's mention on marriage in Ephesians 5:31-32, it implies that the first prophetic word about Jesus touches the very deep things of God's heart—the plan that existed in His heart before time began. The plan was that God would give His Son a suitable helper with whom He could share His rule and reign of the universe.

Second Corinthians explains the principle and importance of being equally yoked in marriage (see 2 Cor. 6:14). The Mosaic laws also deal with the importance of being equally yoked. "Do not plow with an ox and a donkey yoked together" (Deut. 22:10).

When we are talking about equally yoked, we mean a sharing of two hearts with the same passion, purpose, destiny, and dreams. The whole story is indeed a prophetic story of Jesus and His Bride played out. The Scripture makes it clear that Jesus is the last Adam (see 1 Cor. 15:45). We can then presume that we the Church, as His Bride, are the last Eve. In Genesis, God gives man authority to rule the earth and to cultivate and take care of it (see Gen. 1:28; 2:15). This was the main training ground to rule and reign with Christ as an equally yoked Bride. Jesus is called to rule an everlasting Kingdom (see Isa. 9:6-7). He wants to do this together with us, His Bride.

In Genesis chapter 2, God declared over Adam, "It is not good for the man to be alone. I will make a helper suitable for him" (Gen. 2:18). The Lord brought all the animals to Adam to name them, "But for Adam no suitable helper was found" (Gen. 2:20). What did God do to give Adam a suitable helper who could be equally yoked to him? God put Adam into a deep sleep. And then out from the man's side he took a rib, and made a woman (see Gen. 2:21-22). When Adam saw her he said, "This is now bone of my bones and flesh of my flesh; she shall be called 'woman,' for she was taken out of man" (Gen. 2:23).

Adam finds that Eve is a suitable helper for him that he can be equally yoked to because she was made in his image. In the same way, I believe God saw in eternity past that it was not good for His Son to be alone–not that Jesus was not complete in His own right, but He wanted to have someone to share the overflow of His love. So man was created in the image of God, but that image was broken after the Fall. Jesus died on the cross, and in Hebrew the word for *death* is synonymous to "a deep sleep." Blood and water spilled from His side that was pierced. And out of His pierced side His Bride came forth.

As Adam was physically altered after giving life to his bride, Jesus will forever have wounds on His hands, feet, and side. Following Genesis 2:23, where Adam declares over Eve that she is made in his image and likeness, comes, "For this reason a man will leave his father..." (Gen. 2:24).

In Hebrews it says:

> *By faith we understand that the world is created by the Word of God, and that what we can see, has its origin in the invisible* (Hebrews 11:3, Norwegian 78 translation).

Marriage was not created in the garden, but it was a spiritual reality from ages past, describing the deepest form of union between two equally yoked partners. This unseen spiritual reality has its physical expression in the garden in the lives of Adam and Eve, but its origin was in the invisible realm. Its highest purpose was to be a prophetic image of how at the end of the age there would be another wedding. This time it would be between humanity—the purchased Bride—and the Son of God. So human history starts with a wedding and ends with a wedding (see Rev. 19:7-9).

THE BRIDAL THEME IN THE OLD TESTAMENT

Throughout Israel's history, the image of a bride is a main theme. We see how God looks to Israel as His wife. But she turns away, again and again, from His invitation to intimacy and instead takes other lovers, in the form of idolatry. God used the life of the prophet Hosea with his wife as a picture to show the infidelity of His Bride, Israel.

> *When the Lord began to speak through Hosea, the Lord said to him, "Go, take to yourself an adulterous wife and children of unfaithfulness, because the land is guilty of the vilest adultery in departing from the Lord"* (Hosea 1:2).

But then in Hosea chapter 2, there is a great promise, which we believe is yet to be fulfilled.

> *"In that day," declares the Lord, "you will call Me 'my husband'; you will no longer call Me 'my master'"* (Hosea 2:16).

"In that day" refers to the day of the Lord, which could also be the day of His wedding because the Lord's day is really His wedding day. In that day and the time prior to it, the Church will have come to the understanding of herself as the Bride, calling Jesus her Husband.

In Ezekiel 16:7-14, we see another picture of Israel as the betrothed one of the Lord. These verses describe how Israel grew from being a child to becoming a mature bride.

"I made you grow like a plant of the field. You grew up and developed and became the most beautiful of jewels…Later I passed by, and when I looked at you and saw that you were old enough for love, I spread the corner of My garment over you and covered your nakedness. I gave you My solemn oath and entered into a covenant with you, declares the Sovereign Lord, and you became Mine" (Ezekiel 16:7-8).

The Message version of the Bible uses the words, "and entered the covenant of marriage with you" (Ezek. 16:8 TM). Here, we see that the Lord has been waiting for her to mature and to come to the place where she is old enough for love. She needs to mature so that she can enter into a deeper realm of her relationship with God not just as a Father but also as a Lover because children have no capacity for romantic love. As children, we learn to know the father heart of God. That is fundamental; but as we grow up, God is longing to reveal to us His bridegroom heart. We have to be old enough to understand love.

As we are entering the end of the age, God is longing for His Church to reach maturity and to understand this truth. Ephesians chapter 4 talks about how the five-fold ministry gifts are given to the Body of Christ so that we may be built up, reach unity, and become mature (see Eph. 4:11-13). As we enter the bridal season, just before the wedding day, I believe He will do the same as He did with Israel in the Old Covenant, when she responded to Him as God, the Bridegroom.

"So you were adorned with gold and silver; your clothes were of fine linen and costly fabric and embroidered cloth. Your food was fine flour, honey and olive oil. You became very beautiful and rose to be a queen. Your fame spread to the nations on account of your beauty, because the splendor I had given you made your beauty perfect, declares the Sovereign Lord" (Ezekiel 16:13-14).

If the Lord could do this with His people in the Old Covenant, as they responded to His invitation to romantic love, how could He not do that with His people, His Bride, as she becomes old enough and awakens to romantic love? As that day happens she will call the Lord, "my husband," according to the prophetic word from Hosea (see Hos. 2:16). And the world will stand in amazement as it sees the

Church, the Bride, the coming queen of the universe, shining forth in all her beauty.

In the middle of the Bible we have the Song of Solomon, which I believe is also the song of the Lamb mentioned in Revelation 15:3. This could also be the marriage song that will be sung at the wedding supper of the Lamb. What is it that makes this book so special? Well, it is after all a love story. It is a love story we all have become a part of.

If this is true, then looking at the natural, as a woman who is engaged to be married, what would be one of the most romantic things your husband-to-be could do for you? There are quite a few things he could do, but certainly one of the most romantic things would be to write you a love song expressing his deepest feelings and emotions for you. After writing this love song, he could then sing it for you.

Isn't it true that this would touch your heart in a way that almost nothing else could do? Am I right to say that of all the letters you might receive from him, this is the one you would keep dearest to your heart, and every time you feel discouraged you would take out that song and read it again?

The Song of Solomon, which is also called the Song of Songs, is a book whose name implies that there is no song greater than this–the greatest of all love songs written. Through the ages, lovers have always written love songs to each other. Today, we are bombarded with love songs from the music industry, and even if many of them are silly, they depict the cry of the human heart to love and be loved in return. If this is true in the natural, how much more has the Lover of the ages also written a love song to His beloved to sing to her. The Scripture says that we have a singing God (see Zeph. 3:17).

It is interesting to note that Jesus the Lamb was slain during Passover. That is the time that the Song of Solomon is sung in the temple. Even if it is not on the exact day Jesus died, it is during Passover that it is sung in the temple. It is almost as if He died to the tune of His own love song–the song of the Lamb–as He hung there on the cross being slain as the Lamb. If that is not love, then what is love? As He took His last breath, He said, "It is finished"

(John 19:30). As He did that, He was thinking of His bride, because in Hebrew, *finished* can also mean "bride" as I have already
mentioned.

The Song of Solomon is like a Cinderella story. It depicts the love
story of Solomon, a king who fell in love with a maidservant, a Shul-
lamite. And it reflects the ultimate Cinderella story, which we all
have become a part of. Isn't it interesting how the Cinderella story is
almost universally known? It is there to point us toward the ultimate
Cinderella story, and our ultimate calling as the "Princess Bride" of
the universe. This is just a rough overview of the bridal message. I
encourage you to start your own study. The Bible characters Re-
becca, Esther, and Ruth are also modeling the Bride.

THE BRIDAL THEME IN THE NEW TESTAMENT

Looking at the New Testament, we can also see how this bridal
theme unfolds from beginning to end. John the Baptist described
himself as the friend of the Bridegroom (Jesus). Though John is part
of the Bride, as the friend of the Bridegroom his task is to help prepare the Bride. John says:

> *"I am not the Christ but am sent ahead of Him." The bride belongs
> to the bridegroom. The friend who attends the bridegroom waits and
> listens for Him...* (John 3:28-29).

Just as John is a friend of the Bridegroom preparing the Bride in
his time, so God will raise up in this generation His friends who will
prepare His Bride.

The life and ministry of Jesus explicitly show the bridal theme.
First, we see it occur when He launched His ministry at the wedding
at Cana. His first miracle was at a wedding.

When asked by His mother to perform a miracle, even though it
was "not yet His time" He still did it (see John 2:4). John chapter 2
says, "This, the first of His miraculous signs, Jesus performed in
Cana of Galilee. He thus revealed His glory, and His disciples put
their faith in Him" (John 2:11). It was at a wedding where they first

saw His glory, and put their faith in Him. Do you think that this was a coincidence?

Looking at the Jewish wedding tradition, the man comes to the home of his coming bride and first pays the bridal price. Jesus did this not with silver or gold, but with His own precious blood. Then in the Jewish tradition the bridegroom will go back to his father's house to prepare a house for himself and his coming bride. When his father tells him it is finished, he will go back to his bride's home and take her. In the meantime, the bride has been waiting for her bridegroom and preparing her wedding dress, so that she will be ready when he arrives. But before he leaves his bride—to go and build the house for her—they first have the engagement meal or the banquet of wine.

The highlight of the evening is when the bridegroom pours wine into a glass and puts it on the table for all to see. The glass stands there waiting for the bride to come forth and drink from it. The glass of wine represents the bridegroom with all that he is. And as she comes forth, takes the glass, and drinks the wine, she is actually saying, "I accept your marriage proposal, and I accept you with all that you are—symbolized by this wine that I am now drinking."

In the same way, during the Last Supper—which was Jesus' engagement meal with His Bride—He put forth a glass of wine, saying, "This is My blood" (see Luke 22:20). I could imagine Him thinking, "This glass of wine represents Me. When you drink it, you are actually saying, 'I accept You, with all that You are and all You have done for me. I now belong to You.'"

We have to understand that when Jesus said, "I am going away to prepare a place for you," He said it as a Bridegroom to His coming Bride, fully aware of the Jewish wedding tradition (see John 14:2). When He poured the wine in the glass at the Last Supper, He did it as a bridegroom, fully aware of the engagement meal.

In Jesus' last public teaching He says, "The kingdom of heaven is like a king who prepared a wedding banquet for his son" (Matt. 22:2). And in verse 4, He tells us how we should preach, "Tell those who have been invited that I have prepared my dinner: My oxen and fattened cattle have been butchered, and everything is ready. Come to the wedding banquet" (Matt. 22:4).

This is what we can call wedding evangelism, "Come to the wedding banquet" (Matt. 22:4). In Jesus' final private teaching He talks about the endtimes. (See Matthew chapter 24.) Then He continues in Matthew chapter 25 saying "at that time," which means at the end of the age because that is what He was talking about throughout chapter 24. Jesus says, "At that time the kingdom of heaven will be like ten virgins who took their lamps and went out to meet the bridegroom" (Matt. 25:1). Jesus is saying during this time prior to His Second Coming, the focus of the kingdom message will be the bridal message—the Bride preparing to meet her Bridegroom.

Looking at Paul's letters we also find the bridal paradigm. Paul says very clearly in Second Corinthians, "I am jealous for you with a godly jealousy. I promised you to one husband, to Christ, so that I might present you as a pure virgin to Him" (2 Cor. 11:2). In this verse, the *Amplified Bible* uses the word *betrothed* instead of *promised.*

Paul Billheimer, in his book, *Destined for the Throne,* says:

> If one wants to know the meaning and the purpose of history, he must look at the end, the final outcome, the net result. Since prophecy is history written in advance, we have history's final chapters in the Book of Revelation. Turning to the closing pages, what emerges as the finishing product of the ages? It is one thing and one alone: the Eternal Companion of the God-Man. The final and ultimate outcome and goal of events from eternity to eternity, the finished product of all the ages, is the spotless Bride of Christ, united with Him in wedded bliss at the Marriage Supper of the Lamb. And seated with her heavenly Bridegroom upon the throne of the universe—ruling and reigning with Him over an ever increasing and expanding Kingdom. He entered the stream of human history for this one purpose, to claim His Beloved....

Creation has no other aim. History has no other goal. From before the foundation of the world until the dawn of the eternal ages God has been working toward one grand event, one supreme end—the glorious wedding of His Son, the Marriage Supper of the Lamb.[2]

Finally, we arrive at the last chapter of the Bible where we find the Church now as the mature Bride in her bridal identity. Just before the wedding, she lifts her head toward Heaven, and in union with the Spirit utters, "Come" (see Rev. 22:17).

Regarding Revelation 22:17, Mike Bickle shares the following:

The Holy Spirit for the first time in history will emphasize the Church's spiritual identity as Jesus' Bride. This Scripture does not prophesy the Spirit and the family say, "Come" nor does it say the Spirit and the army, nor the kingdom, nor the body, nor the temple and not the Spirit and the priesthood, but only the Spirit and the Bride.[3]

The Scripture is clear that this will be the dominating revelation and understanding in the Church, and it will happen on this side of eternity, just prior to the Second Coming.

It may be difficult for some men to see themselves as a bride, but this is not a gender issue as we are also called sons of God (see Gal. 3:26-28). In the same way, we are all the Bride of Christ, which speaks of our position of intimacy with the Lord. As C.S. Lewis said, "God is the Masculine before which all of us are feminine."

Hopefully, by now you can see that what we have become part of is the ultimate Cinderella story, and the great news is that it is not a fairy tale but a true story. Let me now share with you a present-day Cinderella story—from Norway, my home country.

A CINDERELLA STORY

Norway is one of the last countries that still has a monarchy. When our coming king, crown prince Haakon Magnus, was preparing to marry, the one he would choose would become the crown princess, the coming queen of Norway. Many hoped he would choose someone with "blue blood," someone from a royal line. But to the amazement and surprise of many, he chose an ordinary girl–a commoner. She was also a single mother who had lived a wild party life (she later confessed this on national television). The eyes of the prince fell on her, and he saw something in her that the people around didn't see. They only saw a single mother who liked to party. But he saw something more, and she captured his heart. Today, she has been transformed into a beautiful crown princess who is doing a good job as she prepares to be the next queen of Norway.

Once I was thinking, what if someone had approached her as she walked the streets of Oslo after a night of partying, and then asked her, "How are you living? Don't you know you are the future queen of Norway?" How do you think she would have reacted? She would probably have laughed at him and said, "Do you really think the prince of Norway would take interest in me or even look my way? That is the most incredible thing I have ever heard!"

But then let's say that the person had the ability to go into the future, take some pictures, and show them to her. These would be pictures of the main street Karl Johan, decorated for the wedding, where the cars would pass on their way from the castle to the church. There would also be pictures of the grand banquet hall in the castle, with the wedding table beautifully prepared, and all the delicious dishes ready to be served. And lastly, pictures of the church in all its splendor, where she in her wedding dress would enter. Then the person would say, "Don't you see; it is you in the pictures! You are the princess bride walking down the aisle to be united in marriage with your prince."

If she understood and believed, how do you think she would react? She would come to her senses, look at her life, and say, "This is not a worthy way to live for the coming queen of Norway." Then she would repent, leave the party scene, and start to prepare for her royal destiny.

She never saw those pictures, and no one ever came and told her about her destiny. But we have been given such pictures—we have pictures of the streets of gold and the banquet hall in Heaven with a great wedding table. We have the pictures of the Bride dressed in her beautiful dress, ready to give her "yes" to her Prince at the altar.

The incredible thing is that we are in the pictures, and they are real. And we are not just marrying the prince of an earthly kingdom and becoming the queen of a nation. No! This is about marrying the Prince of the universe and becoming His "Princess Bride" and queen.

When we realize the future that awaits us, should we not forsake everything that holds us back from embracing the fact that we are soon to be wedded to our Bridegroom King? We should say, "This is not the way to live for the coming queen of the universe." Then we should repent and start to prepare for our royal role and destiny.

ENDNOTES

1. Paul E. Billheimer, *Destined for the Throne* (Fort Washington, PA: Christian Literature Crusade, 1975), 22-23.

2. Paul E. Billheimer, *Destined for the Throne* (Fort Washington, PA: Christian Literature Crusade, 1975), 25-26.

3. Mike Bickle, "The Church Engaged by the Spirit," *Arise and Shine Journal* Vol. 2 No. 1 (2006), 19.

Questions for Reflection

1. In what way do you see yourself as the Bride of Christ, understanding that this is not a gender issue?

2. What do you think are the consequences if the Church does not mature to being the Bride?

3. How does a bride invest her time and energy when she knows she is about to get married?

PART II

Returning to a Heavenly Mindset

"Don't be so heavenly-minded that you are no earthly good." Is this statement true? And is this the real problem in the Church today? Looking at the Church today, I think it is more accurate to say that it is neither heavenly-minded and many times no earthly good either. Could it be then that the reason we are of so little earthly good is that we are not heavenly-minded?

I would like to suggest to you an experiment. Take an average church and divide it in two. Then have one half of the church take one hour a day for one year to meditate on Heaven. For the other group, have them use that same hour each day to watch some entertainment on television. At the end of that one-year period, who do you think will be of most earthly good in the remaining 23 hours of the day?

I believe it is crucial for the Church in this hour to return to a heavenly mindset. That was the secret of the saints of old, and that will be the secret of this arising bridal generation. How then do we become heavenly-minded in the right way so that we can truly become earthly good?

Closely related to this topic is the understanding of the Kingdom of God! In the end, the question is not of being heavenly or earthly-minded but of having a kingdom mindset. These are some of the issues we will look at further in Part II.

Chapter 7

The Gospel of the Kingdom—The Message of the Bridal Generation

And this gospel of the kingdom will be preached in the whole world as a testimony to all nations, and then the end will come (Matthew 24:14).

Our call is to preach the Gospel. But the question is, the gospel of what? The word *gospel* means "Good News." So now we ask the question "Good News about what?" We used to understand that Good News is just about salvation–Jesus paying the price for our sins. The Good News certainly includes that. But that is not just what the Gospel is all about.

Jesus Proclaimed a Kingdom Message

Jesus modeled what message we should preach. What did He preach? He went around preaching the Good News of the Kingdom! That was the heart of His message–that the Kingdom of God is near. Jesus was preaching the kingdom message, and as He preached it He also demonstrated the power of this Kingdom.

Jesus went throughout Galilee, teaching in their synagogues, preaching the good news of the kingdom, and healing every disease and sickness among the people (Matthew 4:23).

His teaching was focused on the Kingdom. The way He introduced much of His teaching was about the Kingdom. He spoke in parables of what the Kingdom of Heaven is like. In Matthew 13, an important chapter about the Kingdom, He spoke on kingdom perspectives six times.

This was also the message that Jesus called His disciples to preach. In Matthew 10, He sends out the twelve and instructs them to preach the message that the Kingdom of Heaven is near (see Matt. 10:7). And then He commands them to demonstrate this Kingdom through healing the sick, raising the dead, cleansing those who had leprosy, and driving out demons (see Matt. 10:8).

In Luke chapter 10, we see that Jesus sends out 72 followers, and again He instructs them to heal the sick and to say that "the kingdom of God is near you" (see Luke 10:1,9). When He taught them to pray in Matthew 6, it was for God's Kingdom to come on earth as it is in Heaven (see Matt. 6:9-13). After Jesus' resurrection, this was also the focus of His message:

*After His suffering, He showed Himself to these men and gave many convincing proofs that He was alive. He appeared to them over a period of forty days and **spoke about the kingdom of God*** (Acts 1:3).

EARLY BELIEVERS PROCLAIMED A KINGDOM MESSAGE

We also see this focus in the early believers after the day of Pentecost. When Philip went to Samaria, it was said:

*But when they believed Philip as he preached the **good news** of the kingdom of God and the name of Jesus Christ, they were baptized, both men and women* (Acts 8:12).

In the life of Paul, we also see the focus on the kingdom message. The message he proclaimed in the great revival in Ephesus was about the Kingdom. In Acts chapter 19, we read: "Paul entered the synagogue and spoke boldly there for three months, *arguing persuasively about the kingdom of God*" (Acts 19:8).

Several years after Paul had said good-bye to the leaders of the Church in Ephesus, he met with them again and reiterated the message he had preached while he was with them (see Acts 20:16-38). In his departure speech, he said, "Now I know that none of you among whom I have gone about *preaching the kingdom* will ever see me again" (Acts 20:25).

The last we hear about Paul in the Bible is from his time in Rome where he met with the Jewish leaders. In Acts 28, it says:

> *They arranged to meet Paul on a certain day, and came in even larger numbers to the place where he was staying. From morning till evening he explained and* **declared to them the kingdom of God** *and tried to convince them about Jesus from the Law of Moses and from the Prophets* (Acts 28:23).

The final word on Paul's life is found at the end of the Book of Acts, which says, "Boldly and without hindrance *he preached the kingdom of God* and taught about the Lord Jesus Christ" (Acts 28:31).

In his letters, Paul focused mostly on the Gospel of salvation–to establish the important truth that it is by God's grace alone and not the work of man that we receive salvation. But this does not discount the fact that he also preached the kingdom message.

John the Baptist, whom Jesus said was the greatest man born of a woman (see Matt. 11:11) was a forerunner before the first coming of the Lord. He preached repentance to the people "for the kingdom of heaven is near" (Matt. 3:2).

FORERUNNERS WILL PROCLAIM A KINGDOM MESSAGE

Just as John was a forerunner for Jesus' first coming, God is about to raise up a whole army of forerunners to prepare for the Second Coming of Christ. And they will again proclaim the kingdom message–the Gospel of the Kingdom in its entirety!

Jesus prophetically talks about this group of individuals in Matthew chapter 24. As He looks down through human history seeing the end and all the dramatic events that will happen, He also foresees a generation rising up during that time of difficulty. They will go throughout the whole world and preach the Gospel of the Kingdom. They will not only preach it, but they will also demonstrate it in such a way that it will even become a testimony to all nations. When this happens, then the end will come.

> *And this **gospel of the kingdom** will be preached in the whole world as a testimony to all nations, and then the end will come* (Matthew 24:14).

As we study this subject it is important to have a paradigm shift. It should be a shift from merely looking at the Gospel as a salvation message to a whole kingdom message. The salvation message becomes the door through which we enter the Kingdom, and the most profound demonstration of the love that permeates this Kingdom.

It is the love of the Prince who was willing to leave His Kingdom of glory to enter a fallen kingdom of darkness, so that He could rescue His Bride-to-be who was held captive by the prince of the kingdom of darkness. As He fought to win her back, He Himself died. He was willing to give up His life to save his Bride-to-be. This is the greatest love story ever told, and it will forever stand as a reminder of His absolute love and commitment to us as His Bride.

That is the salvation message that paved the way for us to enter the Kingdom. Then as we enter the Kingdom, Jesus wants us to seek further for the treasure in it. He wants us to seek for further revelation of what the kingdom message is all about.

Jesus said, "The kingdom of heaven is like a treasure hidden in a field" (Matt. 13:44). When He taught His disciples to pray He said, "Ask and it will be given to you [prayer for salvation, the free gift of God]; seek and you will find" (Matt. 7:7). We often do the first part, "Ask and you will receive," and then we usually stop there and do not pursue farther. But Jesus is teaching a progression in our spiritual life. He is inviting us not simply to ask but also to seek treasures in the Kingdom.

Let me try to explain through C.S. Lewis' *The Lion, the Witch and the Wardrobe*. In that book, we follow the lives of four children: Peter, Susan, Edmund, and Lucy. They are characters who enter the kingdom of Narnia through the mystery of the wardrobe. When they first enter, they find themselves in a dark forest during winter. As they find their way through the forest, they fully enter the kingdom of Narnia. But can we say that they found it? They were in it but had no understanding of what they had become a part of. They could have chosen to stay where they first entered the kingdom through the wardrobe and that would have been all they had known. But instead they chose to explore the kingdom of Narnia. And what they found was something beyond their wildest dreams and imagination.

In the same way, as we enter this Kingdom Jesus wants us to go and explore this vast and great Kingdom and to discover its treasures and secrets. Finding this Kingdom is really the first step to unearthing what the message of the Kingdom is all about.

And who will find it? It will be treasure hunters, and these treasure hunters are forceful.

> *From the days of John the Baptist until now, the kingdom of heaven has been forcefully advancing, and forceful men lay hold of it* (Matthew 11:12).

Jesus is talking about a group of people whom He describes as forceful. What are they doing? Laying hold of the Kingdom. And what does it mean to be forceful? Is it to pray the loudest in a prayer meeting? One way to be forceful is to live a fasted lifestyle. As you fast, you become forceful. You are forceful with your own body, telling it who is in control.

In Matthew chapter 13, it states:

> *Therefore every teacher of the law who has been instructed about the kingdom of heaven is like the owner of a house who brings out of his storeroom new treasures as well as old* (Matthew 13:52).

As we find this Kingdom and receive instruction and teaching about it, we become like the owner of a storehouse of treasures—both old and new—that we can share with others. Some are old treasures that others have found and instructed and told us about, and some are new that we went out and found all by ourselves—revelation given to us straight from Heaven not through some of His other vessels.

WHAT IS THE KINGDOM MESSAGE?

So what then is the message of the Kingdom? Rick Joyner answers that question in his book, *A Prophetic Vision for the 21st Century*:

> The message Jesus preached was not the gospel of salvation, although that was contained in His message. Neither was His message about the church. In all of His messages, He only made a few brief references to the church.
>
> His message was *the kingdom*, and this is the message we have been given to preach. This does not belittle the importance of our salvation, nor negate the high place of the church in His plan. However, the message of the kingdom is bigger than these. Great truths are included in the message of the kingdom, but they are never intended to eclipse it.
>
> The message of the kingdom is essentially one basic but all-encompassing truth—Jesus is the King! He reigns, and His kingdom will be an everlasting kingdom.[1]

The message of the Kingdom is the message of the King and His Kingdom. It is the message of the throne from which He rules and that He wants to offer His Son. But it also includes His dream, to give His Son a Bride who can join Him on the throne so that they can rule and reign this Kingdom. It's an eternal Kingdom, and there is no place in this vast universe that His Kingdom is not ruling, except one tiny planet on the outskirts of the universe—earth.

The Bible tells us that the earth "is under the control of the evil one" (1 John 5:19). This world has rebelled against the King and His Kingdom and is now being ruled by the king of darkness or the ruler of the kingdom of the air. He has taken the inhabitants of this world under his control. As it says in Ephesians:

> *As for you, you were dead in your transgressions and sins, in which you used to live when you followed the ways of this world and of the ruler of the kingdom of the air, the spirit who is now at work in those who are disobedient* (Ephesians 2:1-2).

We were the slaves of this evil ruler and the evil principalities of his kingdom. But then, like the inhabitants of Narnia—who whispered to each other that one day the Lion Aslan would come to restore his righteous reign, and the winter would be over and gone—we also now share the Good News of His coming Kingdom, which will soon fully come to this dark and fallen world. As it says in Colossians, we will be:

> *Giving thanks to the Father, who has qualified you to share in the inheritance of the saints in the kingdom of light. For He has rescued us from the dominion of darkness and brought us into the kingdom of the Son He loves, in whom we have redemption, the forgiveness of sins* (Colossians 1:12-14).

As we receive the forgiveness of sins, we are born again as citizens of a totally new Kingdom. We go from the kingdom of darkness to the Kingdom of light. Now, we are being prepared for the ultimate battle of these two opposing kingdoms.

This is our hope and glory: for the day when His Kingdom of light will fully reign forever and ever.

> *The seventh angel sounded his trumpet, and there were loud voices in heaven, which said: "The kingdom of the world has become the kingdom of our Lord and of His Christ, and He will reign for ever and ever"* (Revelation 11:15).

Jesus, in talking about this day, says:

When these things begin to take place, stand up and lift up your heads, because your redemption is drawing near...Even so, when you see these things happening, you know that the kingdom of God is near (Luke 21:28,31).

So the Good News of the Kingdom is the Good News of the all powerful, beautiful King—who has an everlasting Kingdom of light, and who did not leave us in darkness. He sent His only Son to this world that had rebelled against Him, so that people could enter His Kingdom now, even if it had not yet fully come. The Good News is that one day His Kingdom will come in its fullness—to return peace, order, and harmony to the world.

Jesus did not only come to restore us to fellowship with Him, but also restore us to our original mandate in ruling the earth—His Kingdom. If Adam and Eve had not failed in the garden, life would have continued as designed, and they would have filled the earth and ruled over it. The world then, would have developed and grown in all spheres of life.

God's eternal plan for man is still for Him to rule the earth for all eternity. Then we will not just be children of God, but also be the Bride of Christ. And when His Kingdom has been fully restored and the winter of this fallen world has come to an end, we will be sitting on thrones ruling with Him over His eternal Kingdom. That certainly is *Good News.* That is the *Good News of the Kingdom.*

ENDNOTE

1. Rick Joyner, *A Prophetic Vision for the 21st Century* (Nashville, TN: Thomas Nelson, Inc., 1999), 166.

Questions for Reflection

1. How should we present the Gospel to our generation to bring them to the Kingdom of God?

2. What is the difference between the Good News of salvation and the Gospel of the Kingdom?

3. What do you think would be the result if we preach the entire Gospel of the Kingdom rather than just sharing the Good News of salvation?

Chapter 8

THE THRONE AND THE THRONE ROOM—THE DESTINY OF THE BRIDAL GENERATION

Let us then approach the throne of grace with confidence, so that we may receive mercy and find grace to help us in our time of need (Hebrews 4:16).

Let me take you to the most exhilarating, breathtaking, and beautiful place in the universe. This vast expanse is like a sea of glass, with multitudes of heavenly beings and the redeemed, and in the center is the Ancient of Days–the One "who was, and is, and is to come" (see Rev. 4:6-8). He is the great "I AM," and at His right hand is the Son in all His beauty and splendor (see Exod. 3:14). This place is the throne room.

This throne represents the power and authority of the universe. It was from this throne that the words "Let there be light" came out; "and there was light" (see Gen. 1:3). It was also from this throne that the words "Come forth," rang out, and Jesus rose from the grave. From this same throne, words go out to direct the affairs of men and the course of history. Again, from this throne words go out to answer your prayers in your time of need.

Once a word is spoken from the throne it becomes a reality, and nothing can stand against it. It is a done deal. In this context, it is the One sitting on the throne who gives value to the throne. Nevertheless, the throne represents the power and the authority in the universe.

In our modern democratic society, we might have forgotten the meaning of the power and authority of the throne. Hence, we need to revisit history to truly understand it.

In ancient times, a king had absolute power. In those days, the throne room where the king was sitting was the center of power and authority in any nation. The decisions or commands that emerged from the throne were the final decision in any case. In the same manner, God is seated on His throne—the center of power and authority in the universe. Any decision coming forth from that throne is irrevocable.

For a moment, picture an earthly king back in the days when kings had real power. Imagine you are a poor farmer who has been treated unjustly by your local government. Your only chance to receive just treatment is to present your case before the king. However, many people are also making their appeals, and only one plea will be heard by the king. Amazingly, yours is the one favored. It is a chance of a lifetime. You know that if you are given a chance to present your case before the king and he gives you favor, then one word from him—coming from the throne—would solve your problem.

Now, the big day has arrived. You are in your best clothes and somebody has picked you up and taken you to the castle. You enter the castle and are ushered to the throne room. You have to stop outside the doors of the throne room and wait for the guard to check if your name is on the list of those allowed to enter. The guard finds your name. The doors are opened for you to come in. You enter into this incredible, huge, glorious room. You start your long walk toward the throne where you can see the king sitting. As you walk down the red carpet you are dazzled by the beautiful chandeliers, the pillars, and the vastness of the room.

Finally, you are standing in front of the king. You kneel down and present your case. The king, after listening to you says, "Let this man's request be granted." When those words are released from the throne, it's already decided that you will have your request.

You, as a poor farmer, might not be able to enter the throne room again. A chance to present your case to the king comes only once in a lifetime, if even then. In contrast, today we are allowed to enter the throne room of the King of the universe not just once, but always in our time of need.

Let me share with you a story about one who truly understands the power of the throne. A drug addict and a criminal one day came to his wit's end and decided to call his sister, who is a believer. He realized he needed God's help. So he walked to a phone booth. As he started to dial the number of his sister, the power of God came down and filled that booth. Caught by that power, he was completely healed, saved, and filled with the spirit instantly—even before he uttered a word to his sister. It was a sovereign act of God.

Many years later, after this man was already in ministry, he asked God, "What was so special with me that you met me and saved me in such a dramatic way?" The Lord answered him, "It is not that you are special, but it was because of the one who had been before my throne concerning you." I believe that "one" was his sister. She had understood the power of the throne room and had been there pleading for her brother. So as he took one little step toward the Lord, God was ready to pour out his abundant blessing on him.

Duncan Campbell shared an account from the Hebrides Revival, which I believe is another proof of the power of the throne manifested when we approach it.

> On a trip to a neighboring island, I found the people were very cold and stiff. Calling for some men to come over and pray I particularly requested that a young man named Donald accompany them. Donald, who was seventeen years old, had been recently saved and then baptized in the Holy Spirit on a hillside about two weeks later.

As we were in the church that night, Donald was sitting toward the front with tears falling from his face onto the floor. I knew he was in touch with God in a way that I was not, so I stopped preaching and asked him to pray. Donald rose to his feet and said, "I seem to be gazing into an open door and see the Lamb in the midst of the throne and the keys of death and hell on His waist." Then he stopped and began to sob. After he composed himself, he lifted his eyes toward heaven, raised his hands, and said, "God, there is power at Your throne. Let it loose!"

The power of God immediately fell on the congregation. On one side of the room, the people threw up their hands, put their heads back and kept them in that position for two hours—something that is normally hard to do for ten minutes much less two hours. On the other side the people were slumped over, crying out for mercy. Five miles away, the power of God swept through a village to the extent that there was hardly a house that didn't have someone saved that night.[1]

In this account, we see that as the young man Donald prayed for power to be loosed from the throne, God answered him so strongly that it manifested even five miles away from the place where they were meeting. That is forceful! That is what power from his throne can do when it is loosed. But someone needs to access the throne room and pray for it to happen. Let's look again at Hebrews chapter 4:

Let us then approach the throne of grace with confidence, so we may receive mercy and find grace to help us in our time of need (Hebrews 4:16).

Have we really understood this verse? This is one of the greatest privileges given to us as believers; we can enter the throne room and stand before the throne boldly because of His blood.

IMAGES IN THE THRONE ROOM

We are encouraged to enter the throne room as often as we need Him—His fellowship, presence, and help in our lives. How do we do that? We do it the same way we do anything in the Kingdom, by faith. What is faith? Hebrews chapter 11 gives us the answer, "Now faith is being sure of what we hope for and certain of what we do not see" (Heb. 11:1).

The throne and the throne room are in the invisible realm. So we are told to enter the throne room and approach the throne, and we do this by faith being certain of what we do not see. We follow the instructions of Colossians where we are told to set our hearts and minds on things above, "where Christ is seated at the right hand of God" (see Col. 3:1-2). In other words, we are told to set our hearts (feelings and emotions) and our minds (which include our thoughts) on the throne room.

How do we do this if we have not had an actual experience of the throne room? We do this by studying the accounts of John in Revelation chapters 4 and 5. Those two chapters are devoted almost entirely to the throne room and the things that are in it. Other texts to study include Isaiah 6, Ezekiel 1, and Exodus 24, which describes Moses' experience of being with the seventy elders. Would you like to experience that? To meet with the elders at the sea of glass before the throne of God, eating and drinking with Him—that is something to long for. As it is written in Exodus:

> *Moses and Aaron, Nadab and Abihu, and the seventy elders of Israel went up and saw the God of Israel. Under His feet was something like a pavement made of sapphire, clear as the sky itself. But God did not raise His hand against these leaders of the Israelites; they saw God, and ate and drank* (Exodus 24:9-11).

Why were these passages of Scripture written? To help us set our hearts and minds on that place. We are to actively meditate and gaze at the beauty of the One sitting on the throne and the throne room itself. As we enter in faith before His throne our experience becomes more real. How does this work?

If you are on vacation in a country far from home and you get homesick, what do you do? You close your eyes to imagine, and suddenly there before you is the door to your house. In your imagination, you enter and go into your living room, kitchen, and bedroom—you get to see your entire house. You are still in a country far away, but in one way your mind is in your house.

The next time you close your eyes when you are missing home, do not look for the door to your house but rather envision the door of Heaven. Then enter it, and at once you will be in the throne room. He who sits there has the appearance of jasper and carnelian. Around the throne there is a rainbow like an emerald, encircling the throne; before the throne is a sea of glass.

Just stop for a minute and meditate on the sea of glass. I long to stand on that sea of glass. If I met someone who had, I would ask if I could wash his feet, and then I would kiss the soles of his feet. Why? I liken it to people who have been away from their homeland for a long time. When they get off the plane, the first thing they do is kneel on the ground and kiss it. They are so happy to be back in their own country. The joy of finally being home would make them kiss the ground. I don't know if I will ever do that when I arrive in Norway, but one day I will fall down on my knees and kiss that sea of glass. Until then, I would have to settle for kissing the feet of those who have stood there. That's how much I long to experience being there.

We have already entered eternal life. It has already started since the day we said yes to a personal relationship with Him. And for all eternity our most important place to enter will be the throne room, so why not begin now? The Father is waiting for us to enter, and our Bridegroom is longing to see our face. Just before Jesus left He prayed:

Father, I desire that they also whom You have entrusted to Me [as Your gift to Me] may be with Me where I am, so that they may see My glory...(John 17:24 AMP).

"Father, I desire"—that's a strong statement! It expresses a deep longing in the heart of Jesus that we, His people, will be where He is.

This will eventually be fully fulfilled at the end of the age. But in Jesus' prayer I believe there is an expressed longing that even now He wishes for us to enter. And out there the great cloud of witnesses are already before the throne, waiting for us to join them as they worship the Father. The Father longs to have His whole family before Him, to enjoy "family time."

The Scripture tells us that there is one family in Heaven and earth (see Eph. 3:14-15). It is not one up there and another down here. Jesus prayed for us that we may be one (see John 17:21). The ultimate fulfillment of that means the coming together of all believers from all generations at the dawn of the coming age. Nonetheless, even today we can enter that place and join them in their worship around the throne to have "family time" with the Father and experience His glory. Jesus wants us to experience His *glory*, which in Hebrew means the Lord's "abundance, riches, splendor, and weight" (see John 17:24).

Another aspect of entering the throne room is that this is the place where we are blessed with every spiritual blessing in Christ. Ephesians says that God the Father "has blessed us in the heavenly realms with every spiritual blessing in Christ" (Eph. 1:3). The heavenly realm refers to the throne room. So, just enter the throne room—that is truly where we receive it all.

We have discussed the dimension of entering the throne room by faith and the blessings we experience as we do it. But as we are approaching a time of unprecedented open heavens, more and more people will also have actual heavenly experiences where they can enter the throne room, not just by setting their minds on it by faith, but by truly experiencing it. Shawn Bolz shares from an experience he had in October 2002, when he was taken to Heaven to see the throne room. His experience validates this understanding. He writes:

> When the heavens opened to me, the atmosphere of Heaven was thick with intense purity in the air. Many spiritual beings surrounded me. An angel guided me into the center of a very large room, which I realized was God's throne room. It had no

visible walls; the room seemed as endless as God's awesome presence.[2]

Shawn Bolz goes on to tell us about three groups he saw in the throne room. The first one was a group of men and women who had passed into eternity. The second was made up of angels and heavenly beings. Then he goes on to share about the third group that he saw in the throne room.

> Amazingly, the third group was by far the smallest group. It comprised four hundred Christians—mere visitors like myself. These were not people who had passed on to eternity by dying. Instead, they were actual living Christians who were experiencing heaven at the same time as I, although not everyone realized the fullness of the experience.
>
> Each individual was being led into shafts of light that would fill him or her with revelation about the very heart of Jesus. I knew there was an end-time purpose to each person's visit as well as a divine union with the Lord.
>
> Angels were assigned to each visitor, but not just any angel. Many were angels who had spent thousands of years in the throne room worshipping and communing with Jesus. These angels were sent to carry the atmosphere of the throne room into the very lives of this small company. As I watched these visitors return to Earth, they were literally surrounded by a heavenly atmosphere that came from these angelic assignments. The holiness and glory of the heavenly realm followed them back in token experiences.
>
> These four hundred visitors were getting clear glimpses of Heaven. They were able to see into the mysteries of ages and touch what only a few have touched while living. This group included people of all ages and both sexes. Some in this circle were

Christians from the persecuted church, and some were from the Western world. I was surprised to know several by name.

What amazed me most was seeing several children in the group. One was a little boy who was only seven years old. Although it wasn't until I was a late teenager that I had a heavenly experience, I began to see revelation when I was only four years old. Children have the same invitation that we do—to experience the depths of the Holy Spirit's work. In the coming days, I believe that many children on Earth will be invited into a much higher realm of revelation than many of us can imagine.

In the midst of this heavenly scene, I realized that my angelic companion had left me and now the Angel of the Lord was standing near me. He spoke to me about the four hundred Christian visitors: "This is the throne room company—those Christians who are called to see and better understand the high calling of eternity, and to bring that message back to the world. What they've seen will set them apart, and it will provoke many to jealousy, yearning for a glimpse...."

Even though we numbered only four hundred, the angel said this company would soon multiply; it is the Father's goal to have a whole generation of heavenly minded believers who long for Jesus to return to Earth and claim His reward. Therefore, in our generation an access would be given to encounter Heaven experientially by the Spirit of Revelation.[3]

Not long ago, while I was attending a conference at a church in the Philippines, the church pastor shared about a revival among the children and youth that had happened in their school. The pastor said that almost half of the children had heavenly experiences and even more had seen angels. This revival was featured twice on "The 700 Club" of the Christian Broadcasting Network (CBN-Asia) that was aired internationally. Furthermore, the pastor shared that there was a prophetic word in the past that he had not taken seriously. The prophecy was about what God would do with the children in his church that would be known internationally.

I believe the arising bridal generation will be this "throne room company" because they know that their destiny is the throne room of God.

STANDING IN THE COUNCIL OF THE LORD

We are destined for the throne, to have a position of rulership with Him. One great privilege we will experience in the throne room is "to stand in the council of the Lord" (see Jer. 23:18). As previously mentioned, the throne room is the center of power and authority in the universe. It is where His council resides, the place where they discuss and plan how to run the affairs of the universe. That council exists even today, which Jeremiah refers to in Jeremiah chapter 23:

> *But who has stood in the council of the Lord, that he should see and hear His word? Who has given heed to His word and listened?...But if they had stood in My council, then they would have announced My words to My people, and would have turned them back from their evil way and from the evil of their deeds* (Jeremiah 23:18,22 NASB).

The call of prophetic people is to come to a place where they can stand in the council of the Lord and bring to the people of God and to the nations what they received from God. Some will experience standing in the council of the Lord, and they will bring a message that has the power to turn God's people back to Him.

In his book, *The Seer*, Jim Goll deals with this topic:

> The Hebrew word for "council" in Jeremiah 23:18 is *crowd*, which means "a session," or "a company of persons in close deliberation". It implies intimacy as in secret consultation. By comparison, our English word "council" refers to a group of people called together for discussion or advice. Within the

Church at large, a "council" is a formal assembly convened to discuss points of doctrine or theology. Within a business, a "council" is brought together to bring divergent thoughts together to formulate the best plan or way to proceed.

Just as there are earthly councils of men and women that come together to discuss and advise, there is also a council that takes place in heaven, presided over by Almighty God, where we can hear and receive the counsel of the Lord–the wisdom and vision and direction that derive from the council of God. By His sovereign and personal invitation, we can enter God's "hearing room" to listen to the deliberation of his council so as to be able to announce His Word on an issue.[4]

Another example is Daniel who also had an experience of seeing something that seemed like a heavenly council.

I kept looking until thrones were set up, and the Ancient of Days took His seat; His vesture was like white snow and the hair of His head like pure wool. His throne was ablaze with flames, its wheels were a burning fire. A river of fire was flowing and coming out from before Him; thousands upon thousands were attending Him, and myriads upon myriads were standing before Him; the court sat, and the books were opened (Daniel 7:9-10 NASB).

Jim Goll writes about these passages:

The court sat. There was a session, a deliberation in the council room of the Most Holy One. The purpose of a court is to hear a case. In this case, the deliberation resulted in the promise of judgment against the beasts Daniel had seen earlier in his vision. Dominion would be taken from them and given to the Son of Man and His saints forever and ever" (see Daniel 7:13-18).

As far as Daniel was concerned, this experience seemed real enough for him to have been present bodily at the heavenly council. Standing in the council equates "being there," as some revelatory people term the "experience."[5]

Our eternal calling or purpose, I believe, includes being part of this council. Even today we can start to experience some of this reality, as more and more people will be granted access to Heaven and have experiences of standing in the council of the Lord.

I also believe many of the saints of old are standing in this council. One passage that indicates this is from the Mount of Transfiguration:

> *As He was praying, the appearance of His face changed, and His clothes became as bright as a flash of lightning. Two men, Moses and Elijah, appeared in glorious splendor, talking with Jesus. They spoke about His departure, which He was about to bring to fulfillment at Jerusalem* (Luke 9:29-31).

What takes place here is a council session of Heaven where they discuss what is about to take place. In this situation, Jesus wanted to talk about His plan not with any high ranking angelic being, but with two of His trusted friends who are part of His Bride-to-be.

This shows Jesus' desire to work with the human race in bridal partnership. He discusses with them the very deep things of His heart, even concerning His death and resurrection. This instance with Moses and Elijah implies that the saints of old are even today standing in the council of the Lord.

In his book, *Book of Destiny—Secrets of God Revealed*, Paul Keith Davis shares an interesting story about his friend Wade Taylor. Davis write of how Taylor, during a conference, shared his testimony and told about one of the mentors the Lord had blessed him with. This mentor was Walter Beuttler who had a large ministry in the 1950s.

> So striking was Beuttler's ministry that his calendar was filled five years in advance with appointments and meetings around the world. His personal relationship with the Lord and his ministry were flourishing. Yet at

the height of it all Beuttler was smitten with cancer and died at a relatively young age.

How could such a thing occur to a righteous man of God walking in awesome levels of friendship and fellowship with the Divine? That was the very question Wade Taylor asked the Lord…"I have more need of him here than you do there," the Lord said of Wade's mentor.

Somehow, there was a greater need for Watler Beuttler in Heaven than on the earth. This was strangely true despite the awesome international ministry entrusted to him. There was a role and responsibility in Heaven that would somehow impact the end-time plan of God and the harvest of the ages.[6]

In what way was there a need for Beuttler to be in Heaven rather than here on earth, when in fact, he was moving in such a powerful ministry? Could it be that God wanted him in Heaven to stand in His council as the end-time scenario is about to unfold?

What is happening in this council? We see in Daniel that "the books were opened" (Dan. 7:10). Could it be that the books that Daniel saw refer to the events that will unfold in the endtimes, which God shares and opens with those who stand in the heavenly council? As the contents of the books are revealed, could it also be that one thing these people probably do is to intercede for all the things that are written in these books, for God's purposes to come to pass? Revelation 6:9-10 implies that some saints in Heaven pray for the purposes of God to come to pass on earth.

Furthermore, Paul Keith Davis shares an actual experience of his friend who saw a scenario in Heaven about the saints who pray. Davis writes:

> I have a friend who was translated to Heaven. He was shown many wonderful things during this encounter, including a scene that gave him great understanding about the role of the cloud of witnesses.

My friend was allowed to observe two men in agonizing intercession over South Africa. He watched as these men poured their hearts out, weeping over the promise given to them while they lived on the earth. Each was awarded a vow from God that he would see revival come to that nation. Touched, my friend asked one of his angelic escorts who those men were. He was told that one was John G. Lake, and the other was Andrew Murray. At the time he didn't know the history of either man or about their missionary callings in South Africa.[7]

Now for those who don't know of John G. Lake and Andrew Murray, these men had important key ministries in South Africa as they prayed and labored for revival. So even if they did not see everything come to pass that was promised to them, we can understand that they are still interceding for all the promises to come to pass.

We are destined for the throne, and we are destined to stand in the council of the Lord. As we are encouraged to come before the throne and present our requests, some will even experience standing in the council of the Lord. Then one day, we will be the ones sitting on the throne as the Bride, together with Him to rule the universe.

THE BATTLE OF THE AGES

In the end the throne is what it is all about. That is what the battle of the universe is all about. You may have thought that the battle is only for your soul, but it is also about who gets the throne. Isaiah chapter 14, which tells about the downfall of satan, supports this understanding:

How you have fallen from heaven, O morning star, son of the dawn! You have been cast down to the earth, you who once laid low the nations! You said in your heart, "I will ascend to heaven; I will raise my throne above the stars of God; I will sit enthroned on the mount of assembly, on the utmost heights of the sacred mountain. I will ascend above the tops of the clouds; I will make myself like the Most High."

But you are brought down to the grave, to the depths of the pit (Isaiah 14:12-15).

That's why satan is constantly coming after man. He has realized that man will one day sit on the throne. That's why he tempted Eve in the garden, sought to kill Moses, and tried to stop the birth of Jesus. He didn't want Jesus to succeed in allowing man to sit on the throne, which he covets for himself. But through the redemption by Jesus' blood, God opened the way for us to sit on that throne.

It is like in the old days, when there was a fight in a kingdom. People would try to kill the heir of the throne, not necessarily because they didn't like the heir, but because the heir was the one keeping them from having the throne themselves.

In *The Lion, the Witch and the Wardrobe*, why would the white witch hurt the four children: Peter, Susan, Edmund, and Lucy? Because she knew the old rhyme that says, "When Adam's flesh and Adam's bone sits at Cair Paravel in throne, the evil time will be over and done."[8] The witch was aware that once "Adam's flesh and Adam's bone" sat on the throne, her evil rule would end. So when she found out that the sons of Adam and the daughters of Eve had entered Narnia, it became her goal to get rid of them.

Despite her efforts, the witch was eventually defeated. Then in the great hall of Cair Paravel, Aslan solemnly crowned the four children and led them to the four thrones amid deafening shouts of "Long live King Peter! Long live Queen Susan! Long live King Edmund! Long live Queen Lucy!" Aslan said, "Once a king or queen in Narnia, always a king or queen. Bear it well sons of Adam! Bear it well, daughters of Eve!"[9]

Isn't that similar to how our story will also end? What prepared the four children for the throne was the great battle between light and darkness. For us that ultimate battle is at hand, but if we endure we will also be prepared to obtain the throne, the destiny of the bridal generation.

ENDNOTES

1. Duncan Campbell, "When the Mountains Quake," *Morning Star Journal* Vol. 8 No.1 (1998), 77-78.

2. Shawn Bolz, *The Throne Room Company* (North Sutton, NH: Streams Publishing House, 2004), 35-36.

3. Shawn Bolz *The Throne Room Company*, (North Sutton, NH: Streams Publishing House, 2004), 35-36.

4. Jim W. Goll, *The Seer—The Prophetic Power of Visions, Dreams, and Open Heavens* (Shippensburg, PA: Destiny Image Publishers, Inc.), 148.

5. Jim W. Goll, *The Seer—The Prophetic Power of Visions, Dreams, and Open Heavens,* (Shippensburg, PA: Destiny Image Publishers, Inc.), 152.

6. Paul Keith Davis, *Book of Destiny—Secrets of God Revealed* (North Sutton, NH: Streams Publishing House, 2004), 107.

7. Paul Keith Davis, *Book of Destiny—Secrets of God Revealed* (North Sutton, NH: Streams Publishing House, 2004) 127-128.

8. C.S. Lewis, *The Lion, The Witch and The Wardrobe* (New York, NY: Harper Collins Publishers, 1956), 87.

9. C.S. Lewis, *The Lion, The Witch and The Wardrobe* (New York, NY: Harper Collins Publishers, 1956), 199.

Questions for Reflection

1. Read and meditate on Revelation chapter 4, and imagine yourself on the sea of glass in front of the throne.

2. As you face struggles and temptations in everyday life, and come to the point of giving up remind yourself, "I am destined for the throne; I have a purpose and a destiny."

Chapter 9

BECOMING A VOICE—THE CALL OF THE FORERUNNER

...I am the voice of one calling in the desert...(John 1:23).

We believe God is raising up forerunners from this arising bridal generation that God will use as a voice to see this generation come to maturity as the Bride. In the Philippines, there is now a special call going out for these forerunners to come forth. According to a prophetic word given by Cindy Jacobs, "There is a forerunner anointing coming upon the youth of the Philippines that will prepare the way of the Lord even into the Middle East."[1] God is raising up forerunners who will not only stay in the Philippines, but who will go out, even to the Middle East. All over the world God is calling and raising up forerunners.

WHAT IS A FORERUNNER?

John the Baptist is our ultimate model of a forerunner. Mark chapter 1 contains a description of him:

It is written in Isaiah the prophet: "I will send My messenger ahead of you, who will prepare your way"—"a voice of one calling in the desert, 'Prepare the way for the Lord, make straight paths for Him'" (Mark 1:2-3).

The quotes in these verses are from Malachi 3:1 and Isaiah 40:3. God said that He would send a messenger or a forerunner before Him to prepare and proclaim that the Lord is coming.

In ancient times, when a king was coming to visit, he would send heralds beforehand to announce his arrival. This would require necessary preparations—roads had to be fixed, buildings painted, among other things. This duty belonged to the forerunner. He was sent from the king with a message, to prepare people for the king's coming.

John was the forerunner for Jesus' first coming (see Luke 1:17). As we study John's life, we can gain a better understanding about the forerunner's calling. In Matthew chapter 3, we find John out in the desert, eating locusts and honey, clothed in camel's hair (see Matt. 3:1-6). There was nothing attractive about him, so why did crowds go to the desert to see him? Not only did they have to walk for hours, they probably also had to carry their own food. Why was it that they were willing to endure those hassles to listen to John? The answer is that he was someone who had become *a voice*.

People did not go there to hear just another sermon. They had enough of those in the synagogues—many sermons but no voice. What they heard in the synagogues were only echoes, people echoing what they had heard others say before. So when they heard that someone had become a voice, they all went out to the desert to hear.

Even today we have enough echoes in the Church, with people just echoing the latest fads like "G-12" or "purpose driven life," etc. I am not saying there is something wrong with those methods. They are tools that God has given us, but we have to make sure that all our sermons are not just echoes of somebody else.

If you become a voice, people will come since they are longing for the real thing. They are longing to listen to someone who has heard from Heaven, and who speaks what he has heard instead of only echoing what he has heard from others. So if the Lord is calling you to become a forerunner (not all have that calling), your first question should be, "How do I become a voice?"

BECOMING A VOICE IN THE DESERT

You become a voice in the desert. When John was asked, "Who are you?" he answered, "I am the voice of one calling in the desert, 'Make straight the way for the Lord'" (John 1:23). In Luke, we read, "And the child grew and became strong in spirit; and he lived in the desert until he appeared publicly to Israel" (Luke 1:80).

You will not become a voice in the hustle and bustle of everyday life. You don't become a voice on the run. The only place you become a voice is in the desert. It was not only John who went to the desert; Jesus did too. After Jesus' baptism, He was led out to the desert (see Luke 4:1-3). Moses spent many years in the desert. David was one who went to the desert (see Ps. 63:1-5). There are no shortcuts, no easy solutions. You can't just have a famous preacher, like Benny Hinn, come and pray for you and then become a voice. There is only one thing that will make you a voice—the experience in the desert.

Many churches are too focused on trying to get *out* of their wilderness and rush into their promised land. But I believe there are young people who are being awakened to go against the stream; instead of trying to get out of the desert, they seek and embrace it. They know that their promised land, which is the eternal city of God, awaits them at the end of the desert.

This is the nameless and faceless generation. They have not spent their time and energy using the latest principles on how to build a large and more influential ministry, or networking with the right people so they can become somebody—a famous face. No! They do the opposite: they spend their time and energy in the desert. They may never become a name or a face, but they are instead becoming something the other group will never be: a voice!

The desert is the place where you are alone with God. In the desert, there is barrenness—no comfort, no entertainment, no churches, no people, and no food. It is just the raw, hard reality of you and God Himself, nothing else. Being alone with God will help you to become a voice. But it does not happen overnight. There is a long, difficult journey ahead. But if you yield to it, the reward is even greater.

It is in the desert alone with God that you first have to go through the painful process of letting go of all your crutches, or all the things in which you seek to find comfort. I am not talking about grave sin. I am talking about food, shopping, television, entertainment, and so on. Embracing a fasted lifestyle is radical. We have seen this in Matthew 11, where it says: "From the days of John the Baptist until now, the kingdom of heaven has been forcefully advancing, and forceful men lay hold of it" (Matt. 11:12).

It takes a forceful man or woman to live a fasted lifestyle. It takes strength to find your desert. In a world where we are bombarded by everything that competes for our attention, it takes a forceful person to say no to it all and to find that place where we can be alone with God. When all our crutches are gone—when we are willing to lay everything aside—we are there in the desert alone, naked, and silent before God.

At that point comes our first test. Let's now look at the lessons we can learn from Jesus' desert experience. His first test was related to getting His physical appetite satisfied. How did He respond? He said, "It is written: 'Man does not live on bread alone, but on every word that comes from the mouth of God'" (Matt. 4:4). We pass this test by declaring that our hunger for God is greater than our physical hunger.

The second challenge Jesus faced was to not put God to a test (see Matt. 4:5-7). If God calls us to the desert, we should stay there until He calls us out. Sometimes we give God a timetable and say in effect, "You have to meet me and make me a voice by this date. If not, I am out of here." Do not test Him like that. Trust fully that in His time He will take you out of the desert.

The third test involved worship (see Matt. 4:8-9). When all is gone, will you still worship God? It is easy to worship the Lord when everything is well–our family is intact, our body is healthy, our business is successful, and our job is stable. But when all of that is gone, do we still worship?

Consider the lyrics of Matt Redman's song, "When the music fades and all is stripped away and I simply come...I'm coming back to the heart of worship."[2] Only when everything is stripped away can we learn true worship.

As we learn this important lesson about the desert, we are ready to become a voice. John became a voice because he cultivated his spiritual ability to see and hear (see John 1:29-34). He was voicing what he had seen and heard. The same process has to happen with us.

We are called to see and hear about the "the unsearchable riches of Christ" (Eph. 3:8). This is what awaits us in the desert. It is in the desert where we can see and hear clearly with our spiritual senses. Because outside of the desert, we are easily distracted by too many things that cry for our attention and drown our spiritual sensitivity.

In Galatians chapter 1, Paul speaks of how God called him. We find that after his conversion, Paul went immediately to Arabia (see Gal. 1:15-17). What is Arabia other than a desert? And I believe it was there–away from everyone–that God started to reveal to Paul what "no eye has seen, no ear has heard" (1 Cor. 2:9).

I am aware that not all are called to be an apostle, but we are all called to be an apostolic people, or at least the forerunners are. True apostolic ministry means to be a voice, to share what is seen and heard. In Acts 22, Paul speaks of how Ananias expressed that the apostolic ministry is a voice. Paul says:

> *Then he* [Ananias] *said: "The God of our fathers has chosen you to know His will and to see the Righteous One and to hear words from His mouth. You will be His witness to all men of what you have seen and heard"* (Acts 22:14-15).

You may remember that when I mentioned earlier about becoming beauty seekers, I said that the problem in our pursuit of gazing upon God's beauty is the distraction of lesser beauties. Thus, the desert experience is needed and important. It's where we can get away from all distracting beauties so that our spiritual eyes—or the eyes of our heart—can focus on gazing at the One of ultimate beauty. When the eyes of our hearts start to be captured by Him, then the attraction of lesser beauties loses its appeal on us.

We need to ask for the eyes of our hearts to be opened to see and to be captured by the beauty of God. And we need to pray that our ears be opened so we can hear messages from His lips. Thus, we become a voice and come out of the desert carrying a message straight from Heaven.

The ultimate call of a forerunner is to prepare the way for the Lord. I believe God will again raise up forerunners—not just one, but a multitude—to prepare for the Second Coming of Jesus. In Luke chapter 1, we read about John the Baptist:

> *And he will go on before the Lord, in the spirit and power of Elijah, to turn the hearts of the fathers to their children and the disobedient to the wisdom of the righteous—to make ready a people prepared for the Lord* (Luke 1:17).

This is the ultimate call: to prepare a people for the Lord. Another aspect of the forerunner ministry is to be friends of the Bridegroom.

> *The bride belongs to the bridegroom. The friend who attends the bridegroom waits and listens for Him, and is full of joy when he hears the bridegroom's voice. That joy is mine, and now it is complete. He must become greater; I must become less* (John 3:29-30).

John defines himself as a friend of the Bridegroom, Jesus. One of the various calls of the forerunner ministry is to be a friend of the Bridegroom. This ministry helps the Bride to get ready for her wedding day. The forerunner is sent from the Lord with a message to the Bride. The forerunner tells the Church about the beauty of her coming Bridegroom and the importance of having her heart captured. God awakens the heart of His Bride by sending a message through the forerunner, and she starts to prepare herself.

FORERUNNERS AT THE END OF THE AGE

Another important purpose of the forerunners at the end of the age is to be prepared as one of the voices of the seven thunders that John referred to in Revelation (see Rev. 10:3-4). The forerunners will be a voice or messengers of the messages that have been concealed in the past, which will be revealed for the end-time generation. These are the messages mentioned in Daniel and Revelation that are "closed up and sealed until the time of the end" and about which John was instructed "do not write it down" (see Dan. 12:4,9; Rev. 10:4).

Why did these messages have to be closed up and sealed? Paul Keith Davis provides an answer in his book, *Book of Destiny–Secrets of God Revealed*:

> If Daniel or John had written everything they had seen and heard, the precious and mysterious plan of God would have been misunderstood in a storm of confusion. Instead God planned to give a spirit of revelation to a specific generation. This discernment would allow those believers to understand these mysteries and apply them on earth.[3]

Revelation chapter 10 says that John saw an angel holding an open scroll in his hand (see Rev. 10:2). Could it be that the messages John heard from the voices of the seven thunders came from that open scroll? And if that is so, could there be a connection between that open scroll and the sealed scroll described in Revelation chapter 5? It says, "Then I saw in the right hand of Him who sat on the throne a scroll with writing on both sides and sealed with seven seals" (Rev. 5:1). If there is a connection, then this means that at one point forerunners who have been prepared as voices will stand and speak some of the messages found in the scroll mentioned in Revelation chapter 5.

What is it about this scroll that is so special? What does it contain? No one knows what the message in the scroll is. We can understand from the context that it is a document, a message that is very close to the heart of God. The things that are close to the heart of God are the deep things of His heart. They are described as a "mystery," the secret wisdom "that has been hidden and that God destined for our glory before time began" (Rom. 16:25; 1 Cor. 2:7). In other words, it is His plan, which He had before history started its course.

This plan is definitely an eternal plan, which mostly pertains to our glorious future and the end of the age, but it is at present sealed up. However, as this present age comes to an end, we are told that the seals will start to break so that what is inside of the scroll will be revealed and manifest (see Rev. 6).

As the forerunners proclaim the messages from the scroll, their voices will start to thunder just as the voice of the Lord thunders (see Job 37:5).

And he gave a loud shout like the roar of a lion. When he shouted, the voices of the seven thunders spoke. And when the seven thunders spoke, I was about to write; but I heard a voice from heaven say, "Seal up what the seven thunders have said and do not write it down" (Revelation 10:3-4).

The understanding is that the seven thunders represent ministries or people—or forerunners if you will—that have developed and become voices. At one point, they will stand as voices bringing messages from that opened scroll, as its seals are broken. At that time—after the scroll has been opened and His servants the prophets (these forerunners with a voice like thunder) have heralded the messages on the scroll—the mysteries pertaining to this age will come to fruition. As it says in Revelation:

But in the days when the seventh angel is about to sound his trumpet, the mystery of God will be accomplished, just as He announced to His servants the prophets (Revelation 10:7).

I believe the ultimate calling of the forerunners is to be prepared to become a voice. Some might even be given insight into some of the messages contained in the scroll that is mentioned in Revelation chapter 5! As the scroll is being opened, they can broadcast some of its messages. In so doing, the mysteries of God regarding this age will be fully revealed and come to completion, just as Revelation 10:7 says.

Being a forerunner is a great privilege. But it will also require a great sacrifice to enter that place of becoming a voice. Nevertheless, it is an honor to be among those who will bring to the Church some of the glorious messages written on the scroll, which at present we believe is still sealed.

ENDNOTES

1. Taken from a personal prophecy of Cindy Jacobs given to a national church leader in the Philippines. Printed in *Arise and Shine Journal* Vol. 1 No. 1 (2005), 56.

2. Matt Redman, "Heart of Worship" (*I Could Sing of Your Love Forever*, Worship Together: 2000), Disc 1 Track 5.

3. Paul Keith Davis, *Book of Destiny—Secrets of God Revealed* (North Sutton, NH: Stream Publishing House, 2004), 69.

Questions for Reflection

1. Are you a voice or an echo? What made you such?

2. How can a desert experience strengthen your spiritual life?

3. God is raising up forerunners around the globe to prepare for His Second Coming. Are you one of them? If so, how should you prepare yourself?

Chapter 10

EMBRACING SUFFERING—THE PRIVILEGE OF THE BRIDAL GENERATION

I want to know Christ and the power of His resurrection and the fellowship of sharing in His sufferings...(Philippians 3:10).

Becoming a widower at 39 and being left with a son who had just turned two, while serving the Lord in the mission field, was a painful and difficult experience. It is in situations like these that we might be tempted to withdraw from ministry, experience loss of hope and direction in life, and worst of all, even loss of faith in God.

We need to have a proper understanding of suffering to be able to deal with it in the best way possible when situations like these come our way. No one can be fully prepared for difficult experiences such as what I went through. But it is in times like these that our faith is tested. Therefore, if we have a clear understanding about suffering, it will help us go through it and even embrace the painful experiences of life.

In sharing from my own experience and how I was able to go through it, I recognize that many people have gone through even more traumatic and painful ordeals. For those of you in deep pain and suffering, who can't see any way forward, I don't want to offer easy answers. I can't say that I have the solutions for you. But I know, from my experience that there is a way forward even from the most difficult ordeal. I can only share what helped me and enabled me to continue in my ministry, and what made my faith grow even stronger.

One of the things that helped me go through this difficult time was a trip to China to visit some missionary friends. During that visit, while I tried to rest and process my own pain, I had a chance to see the suffering Church of China through videos and reading their stories. These stories ministered to me as I faced the reality of the pain in my own life. The fact that at that time I was actually in China, where those stories occurred, made the experience more moving and real.

As I listened and read the stories, I came to an understanding that the Chinese Church has a theology of suffering that we in the West are missing. It is probably missing in other places too, like the Philippines.

From my observations, I could say that the Chinese Church has understood and embraced the message found in Philippians, which says, "I want to know Christ and the power of His resurrection and the fellowship of sharing in His sufferings, becoming like Him in His death" (Philippians 3:10). This verse has three central points:

1. To know Christ, speaking about intimacy with Him.

2. To know the power of His resurrection, which is the anointing for ministry.

3. To know the fellowship of sharing in His suffering.

The Depth of His Love in Suffering

In the Western church we love to preach and pursue the first two points. But the verse does not have only two but three points, and Paul gave equal devotion to all–including point three, which is the embracing of suffering.

In contrast, the Chinese Church has embraced Paul's three-point message found in Philippians 3:10. It is probably the reason why they have also experienced so much of His intimacy and power. I don't think it is a coincidence that Brother Yun's book, *The Heavenly Man*, became an international bestseller. It also became the "Book of the Year" at the Christian Booksellers Convention.

God wants this message about embracing suffering that the Chinese Church has learned to be seen by the Body of Christ worldwide. It is like God is saying, "If you want the intimacy and power of the Chinese Church, you also have to learn from them how to embrace suffering." Why then is this so important? What does it mean to embrace suffering? And what kind of suffering are we talking about?

In dealing with my own pain, I realized that during the course of life, we will meet pain and suffering. For some, it will seemingly be more painful than others; nonetheless, we all experience it.

Much of the pain we experience is a result of living in a fallen world, and also the consequences of our own or other people's wrong decisions and mistakes. Sometimes, however, it is the *cup* that Jesus refers to in Gethesemane, which has come into our hands. The question then becomes, "Am I now willing to drink it?" Jesus said, "My Father, if it is possible, may this cup be taken from Me. Yet not as I will, but as You will" (Matt. 26:39). "This cup" represented the sufferings Jesus had to undergo for us. When Paul speaks of the fellowship of His sufferings, he is referring to this cup.

In the Book of Matthew, we see that Jesus tells His disciples that they will also partake of this cup (see Matt. 20:20-23). When the mother of John and James came to Jesus and asked a question about power, Jesus answered, saying something like, "You don't know what you are asking. You can't have power without being willing to embrace suffering. Can you do that? Can you drink My cup?" "Yes," they answered. Then He said something like this, "You don't really know what you are saying yes to. But I promise you, you will drink My cup. You will share in the fellowship of My suffering."

Why is it so important to take part in this dimension of the Gospel? It is important because we are called to become like Him, which includes the aspect of suffering (see Rom. 8:29; Phil. 1:29).

Paul prayed in Ephesians that we would "grasp how wide and long and high and deep is the love of Christ" (Eph 3:18). What is the depth of His love other than that He went down to the very pit of hell? The depth of His love speaks about suffering; it is the other side of love. It tells us about the extent of His love for us. We can never understand fully this side of love if we are not willing to enter into a fellowship of suffering with Him. It is only to the degree we ourselves have experienced pain that we can understand the depth of it.

There is no more suffering in eternity. So if we don't enter into it or embrace this reality now, we are depriving ourselves for all eternity. It is only in embracing suffering in the realm of earthly life that we can understand the depth of His love. If we don't embrace this reality, we may be missing out on some of the very reasons why God allowed the Fall and suffering to enter the world.

God wants voluntary lovers who have learned not only the heights but also the depths of His love, which only a fallen world could teach us in-depth. What the enemy meant for evil, the Lord turned around and used to achieve an even greater purpose. As it says in Romans, "And we know that in all things God works for the good of those who love Him" (Rom. 8:28).

God turned the Fall of Man around and used it for a greater purpose so that now the Bride could learn the depths of the love of God, which a whole eternity without the Fall could not teach her. Could that also be the reason why God puts our tears in a bottle? (See Psalms 56:8 KJV.) Those tears we shed in the face of pain and suffering are precious to Him. That's when we learn about the depth of His love, and for all eternity He will have that bottle to show us. He will remind us how every single tear taught us the depth of His love.

Our tears then become the only thing we can bring with us from earth. Jesus also brought something with Him from earth. It was His nail-pierced hands, those wounds that were brought by pain on earth. Interestingly, the bottle containing our tears of pain could be the only physical thing that we will bring from earth to Heaven. Those experiences of suffering we have will become what distinguishes us as His Bride from the rest of the created order for all eternity. Our experience is uniquely shared between us and Him, Bride and Bridegroom.

So when the cup of suffering comes our way we should embrace it. We must not run away from it, but take and drink it.

SUFFERING IS LIKE BEING SIFTED AS WHEAT

Another dimension of embracing suffering is what I call the "sifted as wheat principle" or the "Job experience." As Jesus says, "Simon, Simon, satan has asked to sift you as wheat. But I have prayed for you, Simon, that your faith may not fail" (Luke 22:31-32).

As we press on to know the Lord and embrace all He has for us, there will come a time when satan will ask the Lord to sift us as wheat. At one point, God will allow satan to sift us as wheat. When that happens, God promises to pray for us so that our faith will not fail.

What does it mean to be sifted as wheat? Job's trials and difficulties provide a good picture of what it means to be sifted as wheat. Why did God allow satan to harass Job in such a way? One thing is clear: Job did not get into trouble because of an ungodly or sinful life. Rather, the opposite was true. What led to all his problems was the fact that he was blameless, upright, and God-fearing. Let's look at how God describes Job:

> *Then the Lord said to satan, "Have you considered my servant Job? There is no one on earth like him; he is blameless and upright, a man who fears God and shuns evil"* (Job 1:8).

What is going on here? I believe it is that Job was now ready for the sifting. We see that God had placed a hedge of protection around Job and everything he had (see Job 1:10). Now the time had come when God would allow that hedge to be removed for a season.

In looking at the story of Job, we have to understand that there are many reasons why people suffer. One reason is that they do not have a hedge of protection around them. Sadly, many believers suffer not because of the hedge sovereignly being removed but because they leave themselves vulnerable for the attack of the enemy. But for those who live for God like Job, there is a time when God allows suffering to accomplish His purpose in them.

As Lim Kou says in his book, *Understanding Job—Reflection on the Meaning and Purpose of Job's Sufferings,* the issue is: "Can man develop genuine, deep moral qualities within and have genuine deep love for God and the truth, independent of and whatever the outward circumstances?"[1] It is easy to praise and thank the Lord when everything is going smoothly. But the question remains: "Will I continue to worship God when things go wrong?" That's the ultimate test of the "sifted as wheat" experience—will I still worship God?

As Job faced the first part of his test, we see that he passed it. After receiving much bad news, including the loss of his children and livestock, see how Job responds:

> *Then he fell to the ground in worship and said: "Naked I came from my mother's womb, and naked I will depart. The Lord gave and the Lord has taken away; may the name of the Lord be praised"* (Job 1:20-21).

This is a very important passage. This is probably the first time worship is mentioned in the Bible, with the assumption that the Book of Job is considered by many conservative scholars to be the first book written on paper among the rest of the books of the Bible.[2] This means that the first worship ever written down was in connection with the "sifted as wheat" test.

When we have to let go of our loved ones and of things that we hold dear, do we still praise the Lord? In a way, as God lifts the hedge of protection around our lives, it is like a test to see what dwells in our heart—to see if we are ready for that day when we have to let go of everything that is precious to us as we leave this world.

This is also where we enter the dimension of worship born out of what I call "existential pain." By this, I mean the experience we have when we realize that what we lost was not something we owned in the first place.

After I lost my late wife, I would find myself looking at her things—her clothes, jewelry, perfume—all these things, which used to have purpose when she was still alive, but now they were just like empty shells. As I was feeling the pain of losing my wife, Liza, I realized I did not own her either. Most of the pain we experience in this world is because of the loss of things or people dear to us. I had come to the place where I realized that in the end I do not own anything. I was a naked man facing eternity. I came with nothing and will leave the same way. That's the place of existential pain.

However, even if we leave this world without anything in our hand, we will leave with something in our heart that we truly possess for eternity—our relationship with Jesus. It is when we realize this that we find comfort knowing that, after all, we still own something—Him. This is what we can bring with us: His love and the lessons we learned from Him on earth. He is our treasure for all eternity.

We will begin to worship Him as we realize this, and there will be a new depth to our worship. We know that no matter what we face or lose in our walk through life, by the grace of God we have Him because we embraced worship in the place of existential pain.

SUFFERING AS SHAKING

The message of embracing suffering has a special relevance at the end of the age because we are told that then everything that can be shaken will be shaken (see Hag. 2:6-7). As we go through times of intense pain—the loss of our loved ones, our health, work, or possessions—these are the times when we experience shaking.

Several years ago, I watched a video that shared great testimonies of how God is changing cities and regions around the world. I came across a story that happened in Cali, Colombia. It was the testimony of the wife of a leading pastor in Cali, who worked hard for unity in the city and who was shot dead on the street. The wife shared how she arrived at the scene and bent over her dead husband. The first thing she did was to say, "It is well with my soul." That really struck me. How could she say such a thing when her loved one had died that tragically? Of all the stories and incredible miracles from the video, that was the sentence that struck me most.

Several years later, as I had to face my own pain with the loss of my wife, that story had a renewed impact on me. I came to understand that the wife could say what she said because she was standing with her feet firmly planted in the world to come (meaning the eternal Kingdom that can't be shaken), not in the world that can be shaken. Even as her world was shaking and falling apart through the traumatic death of her husband, she remained standing. Her story became the most powerful testimony to me. A testimony of one who belonged to the world that is to come, the world that cannot be shaken.

Needless to say, this does not mean that we will no longer feel the pain of loss or deny its reality. No, it only means we can bear our pain because we belong to the world where pain and suffering do not exist anymore, and that gives us the grace and courage to move on.

I believe embracing suffering will be an important lesson for the bridal generation to learn as we are facing a future where everything that can be shaken will be shaken.

ENDNOTES

1. Lim Kou, *"Understanding Job—Reflection on the Meaning and Purpose of Job's Sufferings"* (2003 electronic copy), 21. http://www.godandtruth.com/gat_books.htm#jobbook; accessed 20 January 2009.

2. Bob Sorge, *Pain, Perplexity, and Promotion—A Prophetic Interpretation of the Book of Job* (Lee's Summit, MO: Oasis House, 1999), 15-16.

Questions for Reflection

1. What are the new insights that you have learned from this chapter?

2. How do you view your own suffering? What comfort do you find in this book regarding welcoming or embracing it?

3. What is your personal understanding of "sharing in the fellowship of His sufferings"?

Chapter 11

Eternity—The Future of the Bridal Generation

...He has also set eternity in the hearts of men...(Ecclesiastes 3:11).

"And they lived happily ever after." This is how fairy tales usually end. This is also how the Bible ends. If there is one place where the expression "happily ever after" is true, it is in the Bible.

Where all other books end, that is where we will begin in this chapter. We will try to peek a little into how the happily ever after will be, although many believe that we cannot really know how it will be in Heaven. Nevertheless, I believe we can know a bit about it. And in this chapter, we will go beyond Heaven; we will explore the new earth.

Earlier we looked at how the Bible encourages us to set our hearts and minds on things above (see Col. 3:1-2). We can use the same principle when it comes to the new earth. In Randy Alcorn's book, *Heaven* (which is really just as much, if not more, about the new earth), he speaks about the importance of using our imagination:

> We cannot anticipate or desire what we cannot imagine. That's why, I believe God has given us glimpses of Heaven in the Bible—to fire up our imagination and kindle a desire for Heaven in our hearts....
>
> I believe that God expects us to use our imagination, even as we recognize its limitations and flaws. If God didn't want us to imagine what Heaven will be like, He wouldn't have told us as much about it as He has.
>
> Rather than ignore our imagination, I believe we should fuel it with Scripture, allowing it to step through the doors that Scripture opens.[1]

It's good to use our sanctified imagination without going beyond the perimeter of Scripture. With our desire to be biblically based, we need to dare to look through the doors that Scripture opens up into eternity.

"He has also set eternity in the hearts of men..." (Eccles. 3:11). The longing for eternity and to live forever is deep inside all of us. The Buddhist understanding of Nirvana, of entering a place of nothingness, really goes against how we are created originally.

The good news is that we are not destined for nothingness or Nirvana but for eternal life, and not just as disembodied spiritual beings floating somewhere in the heavenlies. We are destined to spend eternal life in physical, resurrected, new bodies, on a resurrected new earth.

But why do we struggle sometimes with the thought of Heaven and our eternal existence? It is because we have imagined it as a disembodied spiritual existence. We think of ourselves floating on the clouds with palm branches in our hands. This, however, is not what the Bible teaches us about eternity.

I believe many of us have struggled at some point with the thought of Heaven being boring. But that thinking exists only because of our misconceptions about what eternal life will be. Dealing with the question of whether Heaven will be boring, Pastor Mark Buchanan says:

Why won't we be bored in heaven? Because it's the one place where both impulses—to go beyond, to go home—are perfectly joined and totally satisfied. It's the one place where we're constantly discovering—where everything is always fresh and the possessing of a thing is as good as the pursuing of it—and yet where we are fully at home—where everything is as it ought to be and where we find, undiminished, that mysterious something we never found down here....

And this lifelong melancholy that hangs on us, this wishing we were someone else somewhere else, vanishes too. Our craving to go beyond is always and will be fully realized. Our yearning for home is once and for all fulfilled. The ahh! of deep satisfaction and the aha! of delighted surprise meet, and they kiss.[2]

Buchanan describes how we will live life to its fullest in our resurrected bodies on a new earth, pursuing new things and new adventures. Being able to enjoy deep fellowship with God and each other makes it impossible for eternity to be boring. Randy Alcorn writes:

We'll set goals, devise plans and share ideas. Our best work days on the present Earth—those days when everything turns out better than we planned, when we get everything done on time, and when everyone on the team pulls together and enjoys each other—are just a small foretaste of the joy our work will bring us on the New Earth.[3]

Let me add that our ultimate enjoyment is Him, but aside from that we were created with many longings and desires, and they will all be met in various ways on the new earth. It could be our desire for music, friendship, exploring, reading, writing, innovations, and many other interests.

RULING AND REIGNING WITH CHRIST

Scripture starts with the creation of the first Heaven and the first earth and the creation of the first Adam and the first Eve. Standing together on this new earth, they were commanded to fill and rule the earth (see Gen. 1:28). The same command was repeated to Noah and his family as they faced a "new earth" after the flood: "Be fruitful and increase in number and fill the earth" (Gen. 9:1).

As we look at the end of the Bible, we find the creation of the "second heaven" and the "second earth," with the second Adam who is Jesus standing together with His Bride, who we may consider as the second Eve. What do you think God's command to them will be other than "Be fruitful, fill the earth, and rule over it"? How do we fill the new earth then? Does that mean that we will have babies together with Jesus? Certainly not! What it means is that we will enter into that deep union of hearts with Jesus, which is already a reality among the Trinity.

Speaking of this deep unity and union, Jesus said, "just as You are in Me and I am in You. May they also be in Us" (see John 17:21). It was from this deep unity and union that God said, "Let Us make man in Our image, in Our likeness, and let them rule…" (Gen. 1:26).

I believe this is a prophetic image, pointing toward one time on the new earth, when the Bride of Christ will have reached this unity. The Bible doesn't say this explicitly. But I believe there is enough evidence to strongly imply a view like this.

First, we have seen how the bridal message is present throughout Scripture, and the Bible ends with a wedding. We have seen how the intention of marriage is for it to be a picture of the ultimate marriage between Christ and his Church, As we look to the natural counterpart, we get insights into the spiritual reality. And the highest reason for marriage in the natural is the union that brings forth new life. This is the very reason I believe God instituted marriage: to communicate the deep unity that exists in the Godhead, and which brought forth the first creation.

According to John 17:21, Jesus was praying for us to enter this unity. As the new creation is brought forth, we will be there together with Him in bridal partnership and see it happen (see Rev. 21:3). Then as we are partnering with Him to fill the earth, we will enter the next stage, which is to rule over it.

> *And they will reign for ever and ever...The kingdom of the world has become the kingdom of our Lord and of His Christ, and He will reign for ever and ever* (Revelation 22:5; 11:15.)

To rule and reign with Christ is part of our eternal destiny. This will be done from the throne of David, which will be in the new Jerusalem. It will be the center of God's Kingdom, which will be the place where Heaven and earth meet (see Rev. 21:2). What then is in that Kingdom that we will rule over?

What makes up a kingdom? It certainly includes lands. But another basic assumption is that there will be other inhabitants in the land for us to rule over. In the parable of the minas, we see that Jesus puts those who have been trustworthy in small matters here on earth in charge over cities in His coming Kingdom (see Luke 19:12-27).

In Revelation it says, "I am making everything new" (Rev. 21:5). It is like God is saying, "I am starting again afresh, with a new creation. I am doing it all over again." Then we read about the new earth: "The nations will walk by its light, and the kings of the earth will bring their splendor into it" (Rev. 21:24). This verse is in the context of the new earth, meaning nations and kingdoms will continue. They will come to Jerusalem to present to Jesus and us, His Bride, the products and cultural splendor of each nation.

We shall live in the new Jerusalem! We shall be the ruling class there. We, the Bride, who belongs to our Bridegroom will live where He lives. We will live in the house He has prepared for us and that house is also the Father's house. It shall not just be in the heavenly realms anymore, but here on earth as the new Jerusalem will come down (see Rev. 21:3).

You might be thinking, "But we can't all fit in the new Jerusalem." Do you know how big the new Jerusalem will be? Revelation chapter 21 describes the size of the new Jerusalem. It will be 12,000 stadia in both length and width (see Rev. 21:16). That is about 2,200 kilometers squared, or in other words it means that the land area will be more than 4,800,000 square kilometers. That is 40 times bigger than England. And then it says that the city also will be 2,200 kilometers high, which probably indicates that it will be on several levels.

The new Jerusalem will be the largest city that ever existed. It will be huge; it will be where the throne room is but also where we have our house, and it will be a city with streets and infrastructure. I believe it will be filled with parks, lakes, and other natural wonders. The lake is where the river of life—which runs down the main street of the city—will flow to (see Rev. 22:1-2). It will be a combination of a city and a garden far larger than India.

> *Then the angel showed me the river of the water of life, as clear as crystal, flowing from the throne of God and of the Lamb down the middle of the great street of the city. On each side of the river stood the tree of life, bearing twelve crops of fruit, yielding its fruit every month...*(Revelation 22:1-2).

It says that the tree of life will be there. Where is the tree of life now? It is in "the paradise of God" (Rev. 2:7). And if the tree of life that now is in paradise—the original Garden of Eden—will be in the new Jerusalem, probably the rest of paradise will be there also. So the new Jerusalem becomes a combination of a city and paradise, the Garden of Eden.

We need to get a vision of that city. That is what the saints of old had. It is said of Abraham that:

> *By faith he made his home in the promised land like a stranger in a foreign country; he lived in tents, as did Isaac and Jacob, who were heirs with him of the same promise. For he was looking forward to the city with foundations, whose architect and builder is God* (Hebrews 11:9-10).

Abraham was so captured by that city that he already had made his home there. This means he did not only see the city, but he saw himself in the city. Unless we see ourselves in that city as Abraham did, our direction in life will be foggy. *In other words, if your vision doesn't reach to the new Jerusalem and being in that great city, your vision is too small.* Your life's vision must have an eternal dimension because our life is eternal.

The entire chapter 11 of Hebrews speaks about the heroes of faith. It says:

> *All these people were still living by faith when they died. They did not receive the things promised; they only saw them and welcomed them from a distance. And they admitted that they were aliens and strangers on earth. People who say such things show that they are looking for a country of their own. If they had been thinking of the country they had left, they would have had opportunity to return. Instead, they were longing for a better country—a heavenly one. Therefore God is not ashamed to be called their God, **for He has prepared a city for them** (Hebrews 11:13-16).*

Other Scriptures speak of the new Jerusalem and how we are to have an eternal vision. In Hebrews, we read, "For here we do not have an enduring city, but we are looking for that city that is to come" (Heb. 13:14). And in Revelation we find, "I saw the Holy City, the new Jerusalem, coming down out of heaven from God" (Rev. 21:2). It is this city that Jesus is preparing for us. He said, "I am going there to prepare a place for you" (John 14:2). And this city is where we belong and have our citizenship for "our citizenship is in heaven" (Phil. 3:20).

Looking again at the understanding that we will rule with Him, the question is: who will we rule over? About this, Randy Alcorn shares, "Whom will we rule? Other people. Angels. If God wishes, He may create new beings for us to rule."[4]

This Kingdom will be an ever growing, ever increasing, and eternal one. We see this in the Book of Isaiah and Daniel:

> *Of the increase of His government and peace there will be no end. He will reign on David's throne and over His kingdom, establishing and upholding it with justice and righteousness from that time*

on and forever. The zeal of the Lord Almighty will accomplish this (Isaiah 9:7).

He was given authority, glory and sovereign power; all peoples, nations and men of every language worshiped Him. His dominion is an everlasting dominion that will not pass away, and His kingdom is one that will never be destroyed (Daniel 7:14).

So what will it mean that this everlasting Kingdom is also ever increasing? Two very important verses help us understand the dimensions and dynamics of God's Kingdom with eternity as its scope.

First, in Ephesians it says, "that in the ages to come He might show the exceeding riches of His grace in *His* kindness toward us in Christ Jesus" (Eph. 2:7 NKJV). Second, in the Book of Daniel it says, "but the saints of the Highest One will receive the kingdom and possess the kingdom forever, for all ages to come" (Dan. 7:18 NASB).

These two verses speak clearly, not just about the coming age, but regarding the coming ages as well. Eternity consists not only of one age but of many. Right now we are at the threshold of leaving one age to enter into another. The age we are about to enter will then be the beginning of many succeeding ages to come.

At present, we get a few glimpses of the coming age. But this is just the first age of many ages that Scripture tells us about. What will the following ages of eternity bring? The transition from one age to another is characterized by dramatic changes. Just like what happens when this age comes to an end and the next one begins.

It is like everything will be totally new. Could it be that certain changes will also take place in the ages to come? If so, every time we move from one age to another, we will all be moved with awe—filled with excitement and wonder—because of the incredibly new things God has in store for us in yet another age. As the coming age dawns on us, life as we have known it will once again be transformed to a whole new level. We will enter into something new once again, something beyond our wildest dreams and imaginations. Again our only response will be to worship our infinite God, who will show us His grace and kindness not only in the age to come, but in all the succeeding ages of eternity as well.

Could it be that in the succeeding ages, life and creation will be brought to new planets? If so, forms of creation could also be brought further into new sun systems and galaxies in the ever growing universe. This could occur in the increase of His government in the ages to come.

Why do you think the universe is so large and endless? Certainly it is because there is no end to His rule and government. It will just increase and keep growing.

Someday in the ages to come, perhaps not only planet Earth will be inhabited. The whole universe—from one galaxy to another—will worship God and serve Him in every place. There will be new discoveries in all spheres of life. Then planet Earth will become the capital planet of the universe while Jerusalem will be the capital city of the capital planet.

Life on the new earth will reach heights in development and progress, which the old earth foreshadowed. In this world, even the most brilliant among us hardly maximizes the full capacity of the human mind. But I believe we shall use the full potential of our human mind for the first time on the new earth.

Why do you think man has been so eager to explore the universe? We have sent people out there, and now some are talking about space tourism. Could it be that these are just glimpses of the vastness of the future world that awaits us?

Imagine yourself being in the future. Many ages from now, planet Earth will no longer be the only space to occupy. Suppose you are sent on a mission to a distant planet in a galaxy far away, to inspect and report back to the throne room. As you arrive you are welcomed not just to a city or nation but to a whole planet. It is as if the whole planet has been preparing for your visit. The inhabitants of this planet may ask many questions because never before have they met someone like you who lived on the old earth.

Do you know what I believe will be one of their most frequently asked questions? It is this: "How was it to live on the old earth?" Think of it; we will be the only ones who lived on both the old and new earth. They will love to hear stories of how it was to live on the old earth and how we—in the face of pain and suffering—did not give up on our faith in God but pressed on. Then they will want to hear how it was to witness the creation of the new earth.

Friends, we shall probably be there at the creation of the new earth, and as we start to live there, in hindsight, we will remember the incredible things we were allowed to witness and be a part of as it was formed and came into being.

Finally, they will ask about the cross, which will still be the marvel of all ages. They will wonder how the God of glory could leave His place of majesty, to go down and live in a fallen world, to suffer pain and hardship leading Him to face the ultimate agony of death on the cross. As the inhabitants of other planets live in a world without pain, suffering, or death, they will have no way to understand the extent of God's love toward us. They will not be able to fathom the depth of His love. But we will.

As we share with them our personal experience of aches and difficulties, we will give them a grasp of what the Lord went through because of His love. Therefore, by our testimony, their understanding of the love of God will deepen and grow. This should give us a new perspective concerning our present hardships and difficulties, as we are willing to embrace them now.

Let's see now how Randy Alcorn expounds on this verse from Isaiah: "Of the increase of His government and peace there will be no end" (Isa. 9:7).

> It may be that Christ's government will always increase because He will continually create new worlds to govern (and, perhaps, new creatures to inhabit those new worlds.)...If Christ expands His rule by creating new worlds, whom will He send to govern them on His behalf? His redeemed people. Some may rule over towns, some cities,

some planets, some solar systems or galaxies. Sounds far-fetched? Not if we understand both Scripture and science. Consider how our current universe is constantly expanding. Each moment, the celestial geography dramatically increases. As old stars burn out, new stars are being born. Is God their creator? Yes. Suppose the new heavens also expand, creating new geography in space and ever increasing the size of God's Kingdom. Will He fill that empty space with new creation? Will He dispatch exploratory and governing expeditions to these worlds, where His glory will be seen in new and magnificent creations?

The proper question is not, why would God create new worlds? That's obvious. God is by nature a creator and ruler. He is glorified by what He creates and rules. He delights to delegate authority and dominion to His children to rule His creation on His behalf as we read, "Of the increase of His government and peace there shall be no end."

Is there anything in Scripture—anything we know about God—that would preclude Him from expanding His creation and delegating authority to His children to rule over it? I can't think of anything. Can you?[5]

OUR POSITION IN THE KINGDOM

Scripture teaches us that there will be ranks and levels of position and authority in the eternal Kingdom. The parable of the ten minas, which I mentioned earlier, illustrates this (see Luke 19:12-27). From this parable, we can see that we will be given a position of authority according to how we steward what is given to us on earth.

This stewardship includes our handling of time, money, and talents. It becomes the determining factor of the rewards and positions we will receive in ruling and reigning with Him. This is about our eternal calling and position. I do not know about you, but this is a sobering thought for me. I would like a place close to Jesus in that council that we have talked about.

Is it wrong to look forward to our reward and our position of authority? No, I do not think so. That was what the saints of old did. Just read Hebrews 11. About Moses it was said, "He was looking ahead to his reward" (Heb. 11:26).

As all fathers want their children to do their very best in school to properly prepare them for their future, so there will be a great future for us. Our Father wants us to be prepared for that day, so that we don't miss out on anything that was originally intended for us pertaining to our glorious future.

You may be thinking, *All this talk about ruling—I thought eternity was about worshipping God.* Yes, it is! But not only in the sense that we will stand for all eternity before the throne, singing "Hallelujah" with palm branches in our hands. Actually, when Scripture speaks of our eternal destiny, it deals just as much—if not more—with our task of ruling and reigning.

As Adam and Eve were placed in the garden, their task was to rule. Could it be that as they fulfilled their assignment to rule, they did it as an act of their worship? In view of this, it is not impossible to think that part of our worship in eternity is to rule.

In discussing our eternal calling to rule and reign with Christ, I believe there is a connection between our eternal calling and the calling or giftings we have now. These giftings are what make us unique, and they will not change as we enter eternity. I think that one gifted in music on earth will continue with that function in eternity.

For me personally, as the editor of the *Arise and Shine Journal,* I experience that I am in contact with the depth of my own heart, with who I am and what my calling is on this earth. As I am in touch with the depths of my own being—of who I am and my purpose in life—I am touching eternity (see Eccles. 3:11). Those dreams and longings that are inside me could also be connected to eternity. As I touch the deep things in my own heart, I am in touch with the eternal calling and purposes that I have. For me, I believe my eternal calling is connected to being an editor. I might be involved in collecting writings and manuscripts from both the old and the new earth—to spread around His eternal Kingdom to give Him honor and glory.

The center of the Kingdom is still the throne room, which will be in the new Jerusalem (see Rev. 21). I believe it will include the sea of glass, the rainbow, the living creatures, and so on. It will be the place where we return to after administering the affairs of the Kingdom and probably where we will report the events happening outside the throne room. This reporting will probably take place in the council of the Lord.

Worship as the Highest Occupation

Needless to say, worship in the throne room will still be our highest occupation as described in Revelation 4 and 5. There we will take turns in ministering before the Lord.

Some may wonder, why won't the worship in the throne room get boring, even if it continues for eternity? First of all, the worship in the throne room is a response to the overwhelming experience of His love, beauty, and majesty being displayed there. And as we have already seen, at the core of our being is the longing to be loved and accepted, but also the need for thrill and fascination. In the throne room all of these longings will be fulfilled—externally as well as internally.

The only proper way to respond to such an overwhelming love and delight is to praise God, and share with others our experiences with Him. This could be possible through "responsive singing," one of the dynamics described in Revelation 4 and 5. Our human makeup is such that when we experience something extraordinary, we long to share it with others. Only by sharing will the experience be truly fulfilling.

We notice this in all spheres of life; football supporters like to meet and share their excitement when they watch their team play well. If they have to sit alone and watch a game, something essential is lost. The same can be said regarding connoisseurs of art, car enthusiasts, etc. When we experience something that thrills and fascinates us, we cannot help but share it with others.

This sharing will also take place in the throne room for eternity—in that place where God is continuously showing us new layers of His love, His beauty, and His majesty. Again and again, we will be touched by Him in the very core of our being, in such a way that we—full of passion and excitement—will express our praise to God.

However, that is not all. In this atmosphere of light, sound, color, and His dense overwhelming presence, we will also loudly declare our excitement for God to one another. Perhaps we will say things like, "Did you see that?" in response to the light, color, and sound *emanating* from His being, as He reveals yet another depth of His character. We may even exclaim, "Our God is truly awesome, *grabe!*" (a Filipino expression for "awesome").

Sam Storms touches on this dimension of our eternal experience of God, and he speaks of how it will forever increase in satisfaction and joy. He writes:

> Our experience of God will never reach its consummation. We will never finally arrive, as if upon reaching a peak we discover there is nothing beyond. Our experience of God will never become stale. It will deepen and develop, intensify and amplify, unfold and increase, broaden and balloon. Our relishing and rejoicing in God will sharpen and spread and extend and progress and mature and flower and blossom and widen and stretch and swell and snowball and inflate and lengthen and augment and advance and proliferate and accumulate and accelerate and multiply and heighten and reach a crescendo that will even then be only the beginning of an eternity of new and fresh insights into the majesty of who God is![6]

DREAMING ABOUT OUR FUTURE

Are we allowed to dream and think about our future like I have been doing now? I believe so. This is about marriage: the union of two equally yoked lovers.

In anticipation of their future life together, couples discuss their plans and dreams. Any future husband, for that matter, wants to hear his future wife share what she thinks life will be like with him. One thing is certain: no bridegroom is honored by having a bride who never thinks about their future together.

In the same way, Jesus wants us to engage ourselves in thinking about our future with Him. As we start to meditate and imagine how it will be, we pay honor to Him—our coming Husband. Indeed Jesus is looking for an equally yoked Bride who will share with Him her own anticipation of their glorious future. Wow! Could it be that as we share our dreams and thoughts about our future, we can even now begin to take part in shaping it? Consider this: God brought all the animals to Adam and solicited his input in naming them; God wanted Adam's partnership as the earth was created.

That's what this chapter has been all about. I want to let my voice be heard of how I envision some of our future with Jesus will look like. And now dear reader, I encourage you to start dreaming your own dreams of that future with Him.

If you think the pictures I have been trying to draw for you seem too unbelievable, I can promise you one thing: this feeble attempt to look through some of the doors that Scripture opens to eternity is nothing compared to how glorious it will be. What I have been trying to show you are like old black and white pictures that are out of focus. They, at best, are a shadow of the things to come (see Col. 2:17). As Scripture says, "No eye has seen, no ear has heard, no mind has conceived what God has prepared for those who love Him" (1 Cor. 2:9).

Life on earth then becomes mere preparation for our real task. Our task is to not only fill the earth with the knowledge of His glory, but the whole universe—that His praises will eventually be heard from one end of the universe to the other. Or as C.S. Lewis puts it at the end of the *Chronicles of Narnia*, this has just been the cover and the title page of the real story.

> "Your father and mother, and all of you are—as you used to call it in the Shadowlands—dead. The term is over: the holidays have begun. The dream is ended: this is the morning."

> And as He spoke, He no longer looked to them like a lion; but the things that began to happen after that were so great and beautiful that I cannot write them. And for us this is the end of all the stories, and we can most truly say that they all lived happily ever after. But for them it was only the beginning of the real story. All their lives in this world and all their adventures in Narnia had only been the cover and title page: now at last they were beginning Chapter One of the Great Story which no one on earth has read: which goes on forever: in which every chapter is better than the one before.[7]

A LAST WORD

So why do we cry "Come"? We are a desperate people—hungry for love, for reality, and for substance. We have tasted the futility of this fleeting world, but it has not been able to quench the longing of our hungry hearts and thirsty souls.

However, we have now tasted the power of the age to come (see Heb. 6:5), and we have experienced some aspect of His love, and have seen the beauty of our Bridegroom. Our hearts have been awakened by another world, and we long for its fullness. That's why we cry, "Come!" Yes—come, Lord Jesus, come!

ENDNOTES

1. Randy Alcorn, *Heaven* (Carol Stream, IL: Tyndale House Publishers, 2004), 16.

2. Mark Buchanan, *Things Unseen* (Sisters, OR: Multnomah Publishing House, 2001), 76.

3. Randy Alcorn, *Heaven* (Carol Stream, IL: Tyndale House Publishers, 2004), 396.

4. Randy Alcorn, *Heaven* (Carol Stream, IL: Tyndale House Publishers, 2004), 211.

5. Randy Alcorn, *Heaven* (Carol Stream, IL: Tyndale House Publishers, 2004), 224-225.

6. Sam Storms, *One Thing—Developing a Passion for the Beauty of God* (Scotland, Great Britain: Christian Focus Publications Ltd., 2004), 172-173.

7. C.S. Lewis, *The Last Battle* (New York, NY: Harper Collins Publishers, 1956), 228.

Questions for Reflection

1. What was your view of eternity before reading this chapter and what is it now?

2. In what way are you preparing yourself today for your eternal position and calling?

3. Can you now imagine your glorious future? Does it make you excited and cause you to say, "Come"?

Epilogue

I am currently in Toronto, Canada, attending a conference where Heidi Baker, a missionary working in Mozambique, is one of the speakers. As I listen to her, I realize there is one chapter that should have been included in this book, a chapter I am not ready to write yet. That chapter would have been titled, "Becoming a Habitation–The Power of the Yielded Life." I am reflecting on the meaning of the phrase "Christ in us–the hope of glory." I wonder not only about how we might feel what He feels for us on the inside, but also about how we might actually be fully possessed by Him.

Heidi Baker's own life and testimony are strong proof of being fully possessed by God. Her simple testimony speaks of how she yields to the Lord's will, "just a little life laid down at the Master's feet," apparently having no special gifts or abilities. Yet even with her seeming limitations, she is in the middle of a tremendous ministry–feeding 5,000 kids, planting thousands of churches, seeing many signs and wonders.

So what is her secret? "I am a paintbrush in the hand of God," she says, adding, "Any yielded vessel, any old paintbrush will do because God is the Great Artist." As we fully yield to Him and let Him possess us, no matter how small and insignificant we may seem, He will end up painting a beautiful picture of our life. "My fight," she explains, "is not against the darkness around me, but against the darkness within. As I drive the darkness within out, I can be totally filled by His light."

This yielded and possessed life then becomes the most powerful force on earth to battle the forces of darkness around us, and this then becomes the full revelation of "Christ in us"—the mystery of the ages, which is now being revealed. This is the high call of the bridal generation—a generation of yielded lovers fully possessed by God.

It is an invitation we are called to enter; *Christ in us—the hope of glory!*

Haavard Sand
Toronto, October 2006

CONTACT THE AUTHOR

If you wish to contact the author or to share a
testimony of how this book has blessed you,
please e-mail at:

ciforerunners@yahoo.com

Additional copies of this book and other book titles from DESTINY IMAGE™ EUROPE are available at your local bookstore.

We are adding new titles every month!

To view our complete catalog online, visit us at:
www.eurodestinyimage.com

Send a request for a catalog to:

Via Acquacorrente, 6
65123 - Pescara - ITALY
Tel: +39 085 4716623 - Fax: +39 085 9431270

"Changing the world, one book at a time."

Are you an author?

Do you have a "today" God-given message?

CONTACT US

We will be happy to review your manuscript for the possibility of publication:

publisher@eurodestinyimage.com
http://www.eurodestinyimage.com/pages/AuthorsAppForm.htm